M000298189

*Grief Diaries*

## LOSS OF A PARENT

### A collection of intimate stories
### about loss of a parent

LYNDA CHELDELIN FELL
with
HEATHER WALLACE-REY

FOREWORD BY CHRISTINE DUMINIAK

Copyright © 2015 by AlyBlue Media

All rights reserved. No part of this publication may be reproduced, distributed or transmitted in any form or by any means, without prior written permission.

Lynda Cheldelin Fell/AlyBlue Media
Ferndale, WA 98248
www.AlyBlueMedia.com
PRINTED IN THE U.S.A.

Grief Diaries: Loss of a Parent – 1st ed.
Lynda Cheldelin Fell/Heather Wallace-Rey
ISBN: 978-1-944328-07-8
Library of Congress Control Number: 2015918117

# DEDICATION

To our loved ones:
Moments are fleeting,
memories are permanent,
love is forever.

Charles Adkins
Alfred Comlin
Dianne Franklin
Bonnie Handy
Shirley Martin
JoAnne Ninni
Doris Osborne
Ann Rugel
Marc Von Utter
John Witt Wallace
David Watkins

# CONTENTS

BY CHRISTINE DUMINIAK

# FOREWORD

What is a parent? And why is it so devastating to lose one?

Whether a child has been blessed with parents who are loving, kind, nourishing, supportive, and superlative role models, or whether one has been unfortunate enough to experience the polar opposite, parents play a life-long role in the self-worth and character development of their children from birth.

Our mothers are the first person we see when we come out of the womb and into the world. Because our parents bear the immense responsibility for giving us life, and are expected to lovingly guide and nourish us until we can take care of ourselves, a parent's role is the most important and essential one given to them. Every dependent child is aware of this. They are always looking toward the parent for their physical needs, as well as feelings of love, acceptance, and security.

Whether it is a love-love, love-hate, or hate-hate relationship, our interpersonal experiences or lack of them with our parent(s) shape who we are for the rest of our lives. The good, the bad and the ugly.

Over the years I have noticed that no matter how much turmoil or dysfunction may occur in the child-parent relationship, children who are grown adults will continually refer to their parents' virtues and vices, and how it has affected them. Their experiences with their parents are so intertwined in their minds, hearts, memories, personalities and values, that the child who is now a grown adult will always feel a bond and a link, whether or not they want to. They can't escape this connection. It is seems to be almost interwoven into their DNA.

When a parent is still alive, there is always the hope that sharing the good times, the significant events, and the treasured moments will continue on forever. There is always the hope that the grown child, who did not feel loved or wanted, will suddenly discover from their parent that the child had been mistaken; that they were indeed loved and wanted after all. There is always the hope that there can be a reconciliation if one is needed.

When the parent is no longer alive, those particular hopes and dreams are crushed and ended. And these are some of the reasons why it is so devastating to lose a parent.

What Lynda Cheldelin Fell has made possible in her poignant Grief Diaries anthologies, is to give the writer the therapeutic opportunity to express their feelings. It gives the reader the precious gift of community and comfort. The knowledge they are not alone. That their very emotional feelings do not mean that they are crazy. They are just grieving. The Grief Diaries series help to educate the public on why bereavement is such a gut-wrenching soul issue that affects the very core of every griever, and what we can do to help ourselves and others who are suffering. Thank you, Lynda, for your gift to the bereavement community.

I believe the moving stories in *Grief Diaries: Loss of a Parent* will touch your heart and give you the hope that there is healing to come and you too can and will experience it.

God bless you.

CHRISTINE DUMINIAK
Certified Grief Recovery Specialist
Radio Co-Host, Speaker, & Author

BY LYNDA CHELDELIN FELL

# PREFACE

Whether losing a parent happens as a result of the natural order of life, or occurs much earlier than expected, the aftermath can take our breath away. Whether we enjoyed a close relationship or one challenged by family dynamics, loss of a parent shakes our foundation to the core. While it is an experience shared by thousands, it's not uncommon to feel isolated and alone. This is why I created Grief Diaries.

Grief Diaries first began as a weekly radio show in February 2014. A few well-meaning individuals gently asked why I would want to discuss loss every week in such a public fashion. I graciously replied that grief never leaves; it resides within every breath we take. Besides, I find comfort in discussing the crazy kaleidoscope of emotions with others like myself.

Like all good things, Grief Diaries grew and by summer 2014, I set out to create a national event to bring the bereaved together; all the bereaved, no exclusions. Naming it the National Grief & Hope Convention, I set my sights on April 2015. I selected the city of Indianapolis and a hotel I knew well, the magnificent JW Marriott. I signed the venue contract in June 2014, and began laying the framework of speakers, exhibitors, subcontractors, and more.

As the months passed and April drew closer, our excitement and momentum grew. It was all coming together almost effortlessly, like the universe itself had ordained such an event.

But then the unthinkable happened, an unexpected turn of events at the end of March 2015, that threatened to unravel an entire year of hard work. With just three weeks to go, the governor of Indiana signed a bill into law resulting in a firestorm of protests across the entire nation. The power of social media was harnessed, and the punishment was swift and harsh: a travel boycott against the Hoosier state, with Indianapolis squarely in the eye of the storm. Conventions and sporting events cancelled, state governors around the nation banned travel, and the beautiful city of Indianapolis came to a temporary standstill. Our convention offering comfort, company and hope was not spared from the fallout: attendees, exhibitors, and speakers began to cancel. Fighting my rising panic and with a year's worth of hard work at stake, I pondered our options. Should we proceed and hope for the best, or fold?

Aside from those who pulled out, the rest stood with me; we agreed that even if only five people attended, those five souls needed us. My favorite quote from Mother Teresa played over and over in my head: "Never worry about numbers, help one person at a time." So we elected to move forward and hope for the best.

And a magical thing happened. The exhibitors, speakers, attendees and even the convention subcontractors united that weekend to form a beautiful little village full of comfort and hope. Our sorrow transcended all differences as we gathered to share our broken hearts and journeys through the depths of despair. We comforted one another, swapped stories, and shared contact information; friendships were born and hugs were abundant. Despite the odds, our little convention was so powerful that it gave birth to a village unlike any other.....a village full of company, comfort and hope.

Following the convention, I pondered what to do with this collective group of souls so full of compassion and kindness. Every story was heartfelt, every hug was healing. There must be a way to continue building upon what was born that weekend. But how?

To my mind, there is nothing more beautiful than one broken soul extending compassion to another in need. And it's true that when we swap stories, we feel less alone. Thus there was my answer: A collection of voices sharing the same journey compiled into the same book. It is a gentle way to not only nurture our little village, but also grow and reach others in need of the same company and comfort we found that weekend in April.

And that, my friend, is how the Grief Diaries anthology series was born. Which brings me to this book, *Grief Diaries: Loss of a Parent.* Contained within these pages are narrations from different writers about their journey through losing a parent.

In Chapter One the writers share the moment when their familiar lives disappeared along with their parent's last breath. The writers were then presented with intimate questions pertaining to their loss, and their responses are compiled within the individual chapters. These narrations are unabridged, as every voice is unique. But no matter the age, the circumstances, or the number of days since the passing of their mother or father, the stories contained within are a treasured reminder that none of us walk this journey alone. And that is what this book is all about.

Welcome to the Grief Diaries village, where grief transcends all differences and unites us in our sorrow. Welcome, my bereaved friend, to company, comfort and hope.

Warm regards,

*Lynda Cheldelin Fell*

Creator, Grief Diaries

# CHAPTER ONE

# THE BEGINNING

*Tears have a wisdom all their own. They come when a person
has relaxed enough to let go to work through his sorrow.
They are the natural bleeding of an emotional wound, carrying
the poison out of the system. Here lies the road to recovery.*
F. ALEXANDER MAGOUN

Grief and sorrow is as unique to each individual as his or her fingerprints. In order to fully appreciate one's perspective, it is helpful to understand one's journey. In this chapter each writer shares that moment when they lost their parent to help you understand when life as they knew it ended, and a new one began.

\*

SOPHIE BLOWERS
Sophie was 50 when her mother Amy
died at age 79 of internal bleeding

How do I describe my mom? She was a bundle of contradictions, especially toward the end of her life. Amy, my mother, was born to a very poor farming family in upstate New York. She was the kid who literally got one pair of shoes a year and put cardboard in the bottom when the soles wore out. This led her to be determined that her children would never be without the desires of their hearts. She was generous with those she loved to a fault. I used to say that I had to watch her finances because she would be the little old lady eating cat food while she paid for her children to dine on filet mignon.

My father worked for the United States Government. We, my parents and four siblings, traveled the world and got to experience things that many dream of. I watched my mom entertain ambassadors and foreign dignitaries with an ease that would have put the finest event planner to shame. She always reminded me of Jackie Kennedy Onassis. She dressed like her, had amazing poise and seemed to be flawless in her ability to make everything look easy. Memories of fine china and white linen are as ingrained in my childhood recollections as Barbies and Match Box cars. Mom was simply magnificent when she was in her element.

My father died in 2001 from pharyngeal cancer. It was slow and ugly. My oldest sister and I made a pact during that time. Our motto was "no regrets." Looking back, I have none. I was there constantly for my dad; my world stopped that year. When it was time to say goodbye, I was holding his hand and there was no doubt in my mind or in his how deep our love for the other was. In retrospect, I was afforded that luxury because Mom was once again doing her Jackie Onassis impression and keeping everything running flawlessly. We supported her and dad, but she was definitely the backbone. I hated what happened that year, but I have no regrets. I wish I could say the same for my mom's passing.

People loved mom, but she never fully trusted their loyalty. She was always sure that she was not up to the standards of others. Her self-confidence was frighteningly low. She masked it well most of her life, but toward the end, as her "filters" began to fade, I saw how the fear of what she perceived others' opinions to be had removed much of the joy from her life. It was a shame because it was all self-induced. As I said, people loved her; she just did not allow herself to be vulnerable enough to be fully loved. In June 2014, I received a call from my oldest sister saying she thought mom had had a stroke. I threw some clothes into a suitcase and immediately began the twelve-hour drive to my mom's house, while my sister began her nine-hour drive. It was the beginning of the longest seven months of my life. Mom had indeed had a stroke and would require extended hospital and post-hospital therapy to recover. Again, my sister and I made a pact, no regrets.

I can honestly say that from that point on, Mom was not alone for one single day until she died on January 21, 2015. We battled through stroke recovery, which is a story unto itself. One must experience it firsthand to even begin to understand the trials that accompany stroke recovery. We were two weeks away from Mom being able to live independently when she took a small fall. Due to the blood thinners she was on, we went to the hospital for a precautionary check-up. They found lung cancer.

After consulting with specialists, looking at Mom's overall health and mental state, we decided to go with an intense five-day radiation plan known as CyberKnife. Mom did fantastic. Although we would not be sure of the results for six months, we felt very confident and went into the holiday season with high hopes for the future.

Thanksgiving and Christmas went by with no glitches. We were happy and had a house full of children and grandchildren. It was a happy time. My sister came to my home to stay with Mom so I could go on my annual family vacation between the week of Christmas and New Year's. We wanted Mom to go with us, but she was just not prepared for the amount of "go time" we experienced. Our family squeezes a lot into that week. When I got home from vacation, Mom came down with a cold which turned into pneumonia. It was time to go back to the hospital. Mom was in the hospital for about ten days. She was released to a rehab hospital to regain strength and walking ability. I was confident she would overcome this as she had every other battle. I was wrong.

Monday, January 20, 2015. I was heading to the rehab after school. I was staying there so I could be close to Mom. I got a call saying she was being combative and disoriented. I got there and found her bed had been lowered to the floor so she would not be able to fall out of it or to climb out as easily. My guts screamed to get Mom to the ER, but the nurses assured me it was just digestive and they were taking care of it. After a half hour of watching her hurt, I looked her in the eyes and asked if she wanted to go to the hospital. She nodded yes. The nurses argued with me, and I ended up telling them that they could call the ambulance or I would.

Mom arrived at the hospital around 11 p.m. at night. I remember thinking I should call my husband.. my kids.. someone, but I knew I needed to be alone through this. I did not want to have to console anyone else. Although the doctors kept telling me that my mom was going to be fine, there was one nurse who was brutally honest. I looked at him and asked if I should call my siblings, he said it would not be a bad idea. One of my brothers and one of my sisters made it in time. The other two did not. I hold guilt that I should have called sooner.

That night has some of the worst nightmares of my life. I can't tell anyone about them because I don't want them to have the same images in their mind that I hold in mine. It was not a peaceful passing. I hate myself for some of the things I did. I excuse it by saying that I thought I was saving my mom's life and doing what the doctors said, but it does not change the fact that I participated in the pain and fear my mom felt before she died. No amount of self-talk takes away the pictures that are on a constant loop when I close my eyes.

*

CHRISTINE DUMINIAK
Christine was 57 when her mother Ann
died at age 86 from an abdominal aortic aneurysm

My mother, Ann Rugel, was the life force in our family, and boy did she enjoy life! She loved dancing with my father and they had won many jitterbug contests together in their younger years. She immensely enjoyed their mixed bowling league, playing

Rummy Cube, Scrabble, Pinochle, coupon-collecting, trips to casinos with the senior citizens, traveling, and socializing with her friends and strangers. She loved big band music and especially Frank Sinatra. My mother refused to look and "get old," as she would often say. She was quite the fashionista and enjoyed smartly dressing up and wearing jeweled high-heel shoes, even into her eighties! Most of all she loved being with her family. All of our holidays, birthdays, and special occasions were celebrated at my parents' house. Even when my mother was in her eighties she still insisted everyone come to her home for these festivities. During every family get-together Mom always made sure to take a photo of "the girls," which consisted of my two sisters and me. Our husbands used to marvel and good-naturedly joke at how she never asked to include them in the photos of "the girls." She made my sisters and I feel so very special and loved.

Mom was an astonishingly blunt, honest, strong-willed woman who had an amazing can-do attitude. She possessed great common sense, good old-fashion morals, and an unshakable devotion to God. My mother made sure that while we were living at home, that I and my two sisters went to mass every Sunday. She also made a special trip every Friday to pray in our church's little chapel. She was always praying for her family and anyone she knew who was in need. Her constant and unshakable mantra in life, when illnesses or financial hardships would often occur was, "God will take care of us." And she was right. He always did.

Although growing up with such a strict and strong-willed mother could be difficult and frustrating to an independent adolescent, and I was naturally resentful at times, she truly helped to form the basis of my character and reliance on God in very positive ways.

Around 2002, at age eighty-four, my mother was diagnosed with a huge nine centimeter abdominal aortic aneurysm. Doctors were so alarmed that they wanted to perform an operation immediately to remove it before it could burst and kill her. My mother's jaw-dropping reply to the shocked doctors was, "No, I can't. I have to go bowling today!" Another reason she declined to have the surgery was because she felt like this was really a good way to die. She believed it would be quick and that she would have very little pain. So she put herself in God's hands for the timing on this.

Another factor in my mom's refusal for the surgery was that my dad had passed in 2000, and my mother often talked about wanting to be with him. She understandably, of course, missed her loving husband of fifty-seven years and was very lonely without him. Then, on February 29, 2004, and just days before her eighty-sixth birthday, my mother got her wish. She was called Home very quickly due to the sudden rupturing of her aneurysm while she was staying in the hospital for a different health issue. Even though this shouldn't have come as a shock, it still was to my sisters and me and our families. Words cannot express the deep pain of grief I felt in my chest. The only time I felt light-hearted was when my sisters and I would meet up every Saturday to clean out my parents' house.

When the three of us were all together, it was a bittersweet trip down memory lane. We were constantly saying, "Remember when?" My one sister Debbie had us laughing hysterically when she would often try on some of our mother's brightly colored, retro-looking clothes and jewelry, and then decide she wanted to take them back home to actually wear! My other sister Jeri would join in the fun especially when it came to our mom's glamorous high-heeled shoes and earrings she liked. However, during these housecleaning visits, in the back of our minds and weighing heavily on our hearts we knew we would no longer be able to come back to the house that contained those years of cherished memories after we sold it. So having my sisters together there with me always turned a very sorrowful weekly get-together into an uplifting and magical fun time.

So how did I recover from the loss of my dear mom to find joy in my heart again? Well, in addition to the loving support of my two dear sisters with whom I was able to fondly recall and share so many special memories about our mother, I remembered my mother's mantra that God would always take care of us. So with that in mind, every time I felt like I couldn't breathe due to the deep pain of grief washing over me, I found myself saying this little prayer for help, "Dear Jesus, please replace my heart's sorrow with Your joy." And every time I would say that, I started to feel a little bit better, and a little bit better, and a little bit better.

You see, I truly believed that my mother and God would not want me to be sad, but would want me to strive to live a life full of joy and fun, just as my mother tried to do when she was on earth. And since I am a Certified Grief Recovery Specialist, it was very important to me to have a genuinely, cheerful heart in order to be able to more effectively help others. So I kept repeating my little prayer of desire, "Dear Jesus, please replace my heart's sorrow with Your joy." Then as time went on, it felt as if a miracle had happened to me. One day I noticed that the deep pain of grief was gone from my chest! I couldn't believe it! Although I should have. Though I still missed my mother, God healed the pain in my heart because I asked Him to. I hope my story will help you to reach out for healing to the Divine Physician, as I believe the pain of grief just cannot be healed without Him. God bless you all.

\*

WENDY EVANS
Wendy was 14 when her father Dwight
died at age 32 in a plane crash

Many people may wonder how I remember so much about my dad when he died at age thirty. Simple answer is he got started early in creating his family. I was born when both my parents were seventeen years old, not that unusual in 1958. What might be more unusual is the fact that my parents had three children who were born thirteen months apart, and a daughter who was stillborn thirteen months after my youngest brother.

Dad worked in a paper plant, a steel mill, a gas station and a health club. The health club became a front runner for his long-term career. Eventually he worked full time in the health industry and came to own and manage a few clubs of his own. After his part-time job became his full time career, our home life changed. Traveling to other club locations was part of what he did for a living. My mother stayed home with me and my two younger brothers. Eventually Mom became unhappy and felt like a single parent due to Dad's absences, business related and otherwise. The end of their marriage happened in early 1973. Dad married a younger woman immediately. She was an employee and eight years younger than my mother. Twenty-eight days after Dad married, he died in a private plane crash in the Florida everglades.

Dad's death changed our family in ways I still don't understand. Mom was still very attached to him, and him to her. The night before he left on the trip that would have provided him with a multi-engine rating on a plane he purchased, he was at our family home checking in on everyone. For a few minutes it seemed our family was still intact. Then he left to fly from Ohio to Florida.

Due to the recent divorce and marriage to a different woman, the funeral planning was complicated. My mom had no legal right to manage anything that needed to be done for the funeral and settlement of my dad's affairs. This complication caused much turmoil in our family as all the funds my father had saved were in a trust fund that his "wife" would manage. At thirty-two years old, he hadn't changed the directives to state my Mother's name. The documents read "Wife". This meant that a twenty-four-year-old woman had control of our financial future.

*

BONNIE FORSHEY
Bonnie was an infant when her father Andrew
died at age 41 from a cerebral hemorrhage
Bonnie was 60 when her mother Doris
died at age 81 from colon cancer

I have been "lost" since conception. My mother was one of a family of sixteen. They didn't have much and life was extremely difficult. My mother married just to get away from the house. It was a loveless marriage and she was quite unhappy. She wanted a child but was told that there was something wrong with her, and if she wanted a child she would have to have one soon. After hearing this from her doctor, he went on to tell her about artificial insemination. He told her that he would use a donor from the medical school, and it wouldn't cost anything. Three weeks later she was called into his office to undergo the procedure. Three months later, it was confirmed that she was indeed pregnant and six months later she gave birth to me. Back in those days one doctor took care of everything, so he was also my pediatrician. On my three-month check-up, my mother asked him what color my eyes were. He told her, "Hazel, like mine." She told me that she looked at him and he started to laugh. She said, "Oh no, not you," because she was embarrassed. He smiled and told her that all the interns had left for the holidays, so he decided to be the donor himself, and hoped she wasn't upset with him. He told her that I would never want for anything. He looked after me for the first year of my life and when I turned a year old, he died in his office as a result of a cerebral hemorrhage at the age of forty-one.

Within two years, my mother's marriage had crumbled and she was on her own. By this time she had another child. She married again within the year. Her new husband was very abusive. He would beat me on a daily basis and also put me in a closet for hours whenever they decided to go out. He burned my toys in a bonfire, and things escalated so fast that my mother decided to give us away, to save us from his abuse.

On the last day of kindergarten, there was a car in the parking lot. My younger sister was in it and looking out the back window at me. There was a man and an older woman who was the man's mother, they said they were there to pick me up. They took us out of Pennsylvania and we started a new life in Delaware. We never heard anything from our mother again. They kept telling us that they were our "father" and "grandmother." It was extremely confusing and we felt abandoned, worthless and unloved.

When I was sixteen, I was visiting my maternal grandmother in Pennsylvania. She brought out a lockbox with pictures and an obituary. She proceeded to tell me that this man was my father. Can you imagine how I felt? Everything I thought was the truth had all been a lie. Now, I lost two fathers on the same day. I went through life feeling nothing but abandonment. I had problems with relationships from all the walls I had built up to protect myself from being hurt again. A few years ago I found out that my mother had colon cancer. I went to see her and we talked about everything. She told me that she had no choice in the matter, and had to give us up. I forgave her, and stayed with her during her illness. I got her medications, cooked for her, and stayed with her until she passed away. It was horrible watching her deteriorate before my eyes. We had just begun to get to know one another, and now she was leaving me again. She tried to explain everything but it didn't matter, it was in the past. I came away with a complete understanding of why she had to do what she did. I miss her so much, we became so close during that time and I lost the first person who ever loved me.

I have been trying to figure out this thing called life. I decided to research my father's lineage to find out more about him. I have found the names of his family members and bits and pieces of their lives. Years ago I was interviewed by Tom Brokaw for a show about "Artificial Insemination and Donor's Offspring." I am an offspring, searching for my identity. I am lost. Lost since conception, but I am doing the best that I can. I have been deprived of my identity, roots, heritage, and parents. I am grieving for what I never had.

\*

SKIP FRANKLIN
Skip was 41 when his mother Dianne
died at age 63 from a series of physical issues

My mother Dianne was struggling with several physical issues when I had her come to Seattle to stay with me. She lived with my dad in southern California. For whatever reason, she seemed to be in physical decline and I thought a change of venue would do her good. And I believe it did.

After a couple of months in Seattle, Mom wanted to return to Orange County, mostly because she felt my dad needed her. I had this premonition that if she went back down to southern California, she would start to decline and I would never see her again. And I was right. Within three months, she was gone.

Mom passed in late September. It was a phone call I will never forget. I was surprisingly fine the next couple of days, spending more time emotionally helping my siblings and my dad than worrying about myself. But several days later I faced some feelings I had never encountered before.

One day the thought "Why bother?" dominated my normal ambition. It applied specifically to two startup companies I was involved with at the time. I was CEO of one and chairman of the other. I was the driving force. And all of a sudden, I was lacking motivation to do anything. It was almost like I was feeling, "With Mom gone, there is nothing else to prove. Why bother?!" This inner battle between ambition and lack of motivation continued for a couple of days until it culminated on a very dark day that, through a very unusual experience, would become a pillar of light for me.

I have never been one to struggle with dark thoughts or suicide. I am naturally a buoyant and upbeat person, and pretty much have been that way since I was born. I did have one bad year when I was eighteen, when I hardly left my room and didn't want to see or interact with anyone. But besides that, I've always been the one with a million friends and enjoying life daily. Since my mom's passing, there had been a quiet progression of darkness that had gotten a hold of me. It first started with lack of ambition and motivation. The whispers began then and continued. Whether those whispers come from within or not is unclear. But because they come disguised as "my voice," the tendency is to identify immediately with them. They triggered responsive thoughts like, "What's wrong with me," and "Why am I thinking that? In turn, that fed my downward spiral of darkness and doubt. This was now the case.

People talk about the five senses but that sixth sense, how you feel internally, can trump all five. I was feeling dark with despair, like I had hundreds of pounds on my shoulders. This combined with my sudden lack of motivation, ambition and purpose, created a true downward spiral. And to make matters worse, I was in Seattle on a dark, gloomy day. No light was getting through at all--not through the clouds, not through my thoughts, not through my disposition. All was dark.

I can picture where I was at this moment as if it were yesterday. I was sitting on a wooden bench near the water, waiting for the Bremerton Ferry to arrive at the dock. I remember looking up at the dark, dark sky and feeling just as dark. I tried to pray, to think of something positive, to let some light into my being. But nothing was really coming to mind. Fortunately, I was battle-tough. I had been through enough dark times in my life that I knew I had to keep pushing. There was a fitness of underlying faith that barely kept me on this side of insanity. I was more numb that frustrated. But like the sailor in the storm, I knew I just had to keep holding on to something. Just keep breathing. Keep trying to focus on something so I could ride out the storm and eventually relief would be in sight.

And then it happened. I heard a voice. Twice it repeated my lines, like a director in rehearsal whispering lines to the lead actor who had completely gone blank as to what lines came next. "I refuse to be mesmerized to see my mother as a mortal." It was repeated twice. These words were so different, yet succinct, that I was both alarmed and arrested. I could not help but take complete notice of them. Did the voice come from within or without? Did it matter? I had never heard those exact words before and it was certainly not phrased in any sequence that I would ever utter myself. These were not my words. It was some type of angel-speak. I quickly surmised that rather than analyzing its source, perhaps I should focus more on analyzing its message.

At first I was captivated enough that I literally repeated it out loud maybe two dozen times. I just let the words resonate for a while without trying to decipher them. The utterance of the words themselves gave me a feeling of peace and strength. I felt like that photo in the movie *Back To The Future,* where Marty and his siblings were disappearing and then started to reappear. I felt myself reappearing with renewed strength every time I uttered the words. So I kept uttering them.

"I refuse to be mesmerized to see my mother as a mortal." I began to focus on the words. I knew that mesmerism had to do with mind control. And I knew what it meant to refuse it. The "seeing my mother as a mortal" had to do with identification. Was I seeing my mom as a body that had become diseased and died, or was I seeing her qualities, her accomplishments, her journey? Was I to see her life continuing? Was I supposed to re-identify her? Or re-identify me? Or both?!

To be honest, ten years later, I'm still not sure I've cracked the code as to what that message fully means. But this one thing I do know. After repeating it a few dozen times, it changed me. One of the definitions of repent is to "re-see" or "re-think"--to see things differently; to turn everything upside down. And I began to see things differently. And, of course, at that moment, that dark Seattle sky opened up and a big, beautiful ray of light totally engulfed that wooden bench where I was sitting. It was instant warmth. A world that was totally dark became full of light. I refer to it as my "Revelation of Light" or "Pillar of Light" moment.

I think even more than the mental transition that took place, and that surprising message, was how I felt in that light. In that moment I felt like the weight had totally lifted off my shoulders. In fact, my whole body felt like it weighed ten pounds total. My breath was now deep and full. I was totally inspired. Pumped up. And that was the end of that. An amazing experience that I have leaned upon many times. It has become an important building block for me.

*

DONNA GORE<br>Donna was 26 when her father Donald<br>died by homicide in 1980

My father was an entrepreneur of many successful businesses. The evening of his death, he left his primary job as owner of an auto body repair shop, returned home for dinner and then left again as he sometimes did to collect funds owed for used cars he sold on the side. That same evening he also planned to purchase oil for the secondhand car I was using to commute to work. That evening, he never returned home, nor did he call my mother which was very uncharacteristic.

The next morning I was to drive to a job in Massachusetts from our family home in Connecticut. By this time my mother was very concerned and had started calling every friend and business associate she could think of, without success. As we anxiously waited, my mother happened to open the newspaper, *Hartford Courant*, and saw a byline stating that an unidentified man had been found murdered in a green van, and she screamed.

We actually had to call the police ourselves and inquire if the person in the paper was indeed my father. I'll never forget walking into the police department and seeing his coat paraded past us in a plastic bag. The events surrounding my father's murder were gleaned from our state's victim's advocate, prosecuting detectives, and information presented at the trial. Apparently, my father had intended to collect monies owed him for a used car that he was selling to a customer in Hartford. Prior to accomplishing this task, he was approached by a female acquaintance whose boyfriend was a career criminal that involved drug dealing and robbery, and would go on to murder an accomplice one month later.

As the story goes, the female accomplice girlfriend was "coerced into cooperation" by her boyfriend, aided and abetted him in committing the robbery and, most likely, the murder of my father. The perpetrator was looking to visit a relative and needed quick money to escape charges committed in New Jersey. My father was also a landlord of inner city properties and may have acquired the mistaken reputation that he "carried a big bankroll." In fact, he had just thirty-five dollars in his pocket that night.

The perpetrator intended to rob my father, but then suddenly fired five shots into my father's body while he sat inside his van. He was left to die as they fled. My father fearlessly tried to drive himself to a hospital, but en route, his van rolled into a house. It was reported that the van sat running for thirty minutes before someone finally called the police. Hospital officials claimed that if my dad had lived, he would have remained in a vegetative state due to the damage to vital organs.

*

KIMBERLY HAWKS
Kimberly was 9 when her father Charles
died at age 32 in a car accident

When I was young, we lived in the Lansing, Michigan area. My dad was the only son and youngest child in a family of girls. At nine years old, I was totally a daddy's girl. He helped me with my Girl Scout Brownies, and took me fishing. A lot of good memories. But there were bad memories too. A lot of trials and poverty and abuse. My dad was an alcoholic, which affected my mom, myself and my younger siblings.

One evening we were going fishing. I had begged and begged my daddy to take us fishing. So with my younger sister, twin brothers and the dog, we got into the car and headed to our destination. As we pulled into the campground, our car was suddenly broadsided by a Greyhound bus. Listening to the glass break and seeing everything happen in slow-motion is something that still impacts me to this day. Upon the impact, the bus pulled our car a few football fields before finally coming to a stop. I remember a lot of people, and a lot of glass. The accident had broken my dad's neck. My dad was a rather big man and they had to cut him out of the car. The impact severed my seat belt and how myself and my siblings survived is a miracle. My dad was the only one significantly hurt.

Throughout the collision, I did not lose consciousness. I remember the whole incident. I remember stepping up as the scene commander and pushing my brothers and sister away from the door. I remember watching my father die in my lap. I remember the sounds of the sirens and seeing the kids in the street crying. For me, this was a "hard drive" moment; something that never goes away. And I can still feel it and relive that grief. A lot of people think grief is something you just go through and you get over. But the post-traumatic situation is when you actually have to relive it and work your way through it over and over and over again. And it's a hard thing to deal with.

At only nine years-old, I was face-to-face with death. I had to figure out how to cope and, in that instant, I felt like I had to grow up that very moment. It was a jolt into adulthood at the tender age of nine.

Initially I had to deal with more guilt than grief. Here was someone I loved very much, and who died at only thirty-two years of age. I harbored deep guilt because I was the one who wanted to go fishing. I persistently begged him to take us, so I felt he died doing something for me. And I was so young, I didn't really understand.

I think that with many young people in this situation there is often a nagging thought that somehow it is our fault. As a young child, we try to find some blame in order for it to make sense, to find some element of control. What added to my guilt was the fact that things were not always great at home with my father. There was alcoholism and abuse. There may have been times in my mind I'm thinking, "I wish he wasn't here." And then all of a sudden, he is gone from my life. Guilt emerged.

I don't think I ever realized how much guilt I carried along with me through my life. "Oh my God, I killed my father!" I think it was only a couple of years ago that I finally realized it carried no weight over me. I was a child; I had no control of it. But when I review my life, I see certain patterns that came from that guilt. Even though that guilt shouldn't have been real.

A couple of years ago I was going through a lot of loss in terms of broken relationships, and I was able to see that some of the issues involved this guilt stemming from my dad's death. The series of losses really put me on my knees and I found myself asking, "Why can't I function? What is in my heart that is weighing me down so much?" I started writing and journaling and investigating and reaching for something higher than myself. I had some bad programming in my brain and I needed to get it out. I started discovering some common themes and one of them was this ongoing sense of guilt. I was able to write that I really didn't kill my dad, and that started a domino effect of being able to forgive. And I became more aware of the guilt and was able to isolate it and deal with it off to the side. It took these additional losses to make me face myself in the mirror.

As I now approach my dad's age when he left us, I find myself finally able to share this with the world. I first shared this with Lynda Cheldelin Fell and Angie Cartwright on Grief Diaries Radio a year ago. This was a huge milestone for me. A breakthrough.

Now that I am almost his age, and have had children of my own, I can see things from a different perspective. I realize more fully the huge degree of loss and how it impacted everyone involved. I look at the pictures now and am able to identify with him as a grown adult, and not just as his young daughter. Seeing my dad as a peer triggers things in my thoughts like how much life was lost, and how many memories are lost. And it's hard to deal with sometimes.

This event also started a cycle that continues to this day, which includes my love of performance and expression and healing through music. My dad always said I would be on Star Search and he loved watching me perform. He loved my singing and he was always proud of me. And I always wanted to make Daddy proud. So I include all of this in my music career, which helps me and helps others at the same time.

I still struggle a bit during the holiday season. Because my daddy was born on Christmas Day, it makes it tough. This is something I have no control over, I just have to deal with it. But I love singing at Christmas time in memory of my father and in honor of God who helped me get through all of this.

*

VICKI HECKROTH
Vicki was 5 when her mother Bonnie
died at age 27 in an auto accident

My mother was twenty-seven years-old when she passed away. We were at a friend's home while my father and his friend were out coon hunting. It was getting late and my mother was ready to take us kids home to put us to bed. Back then cars were not automatic, instead they were manual. Mom had forgotten her purse. She thought she had put the car in park, and then ran back to the house to get her purse. The car started rolling with us three kids inside, and mom tried to stop it so we would not get hurt. The car ran over my mother and broke her neck. I remember having a bloody nose from hitting my head on the dash, seeing my mother laying on the ground, and my mom's friend taking us into the house. I remember my mom's last words: she told my dad to take care of her children.

The next day was a blur of people being everywhere. Many were crying but I didn't understand why. I wasn't told anything at all about my mother being dead, that I can remember. I remember she worked at a home for disabled children and one of her coworkers who had not yet heard the news showed up with a puppy that my mother had wanted for us kids. We didn't get to keep it.

I was daddy's little girl at the time so I spent a lot of time sitting on my dad's lap crying because I wanted my mother. I was too young to understand.

*

TERESA HERRING<br>Teresa was 47 when her father Burton<br>died at age 65 from brain cancer

My parents met, wed, and divorced in the 1960s. As an adult, I find it really strange they divorced in 1966. To me the 1960s was still the era of wedding forever and never divorcing. To the best of my knowledge, my father was possessive of my mother. My father would sneak under the house in the crawl space to listen and see if she was being truthful. What has to happen to a person to feel the need to crawl under a dirty, spider-filled crawl space just to see how your marriage is doing? Neither of my parents should have had children as neither of them ever took responsibility for raising me in a healthy, loving and safe home. I don't know much about how my mother acted then, but if she was as she is now, it would have been a true battle of wills with no regard for us children. I would think being with either of them at this time would be a true battlefield with no real winners.

During this crazy time my father met and married my aunt's sister and she got pregnant very soon after. Some say the pregnancy happened before and others say it happened after my parents separated. But it really doesn't matter; what really mattered was that my father was replacing me and our family unit. I have always felt unwanted and unloved; even now forty-plus years later, I struggle. I will always be the two-year-old needing and wanting my father's love and protection.

My father eventually had three children with her. I have only a couple of memories of being with that family. On one visit when I was about five-years-old, I spent the night in their daughter's room and we got scared and ran to their room. They pulled her into bed between them and my father said you can sleep here on the floor. I left the room in tears, he didn't follow. I was crushed.

The next memory I have was around the same age. I was in the back of a police car having a struggle with my mother who was trying to pull my pants down to show the officer the bruises from my stepmother beating me. I remember screaming, crying, begging and I had no one to protect me. I was wounded yet again. My stepmother, I believe, gave me the brunt of the abuse and would always cut all my beautiful long hair off to make me look like a boy and to prevent my grandmother from curling it, which I loved.

From what I remember, my father was never really around after that. My paternal grandmother came to take us to visit her a couple of times. Most of the time my father never came to see us then either. I don't recall the excuses he used, since he couldn't use mom being around, and he lived in the same town as his mother.

I did reach out to my father once, when I was around seventeen and needed money for me and my son. He refused saying he wasn't there to see whether I really needed it or not. I was such a lost child, and in a lot of ways I still am that lost child.

When my father passed away a few years ago, I chose not to go to the funeral home or even his service. I went back and forth and in the end decided he didn't deserve my respect. I was not part of his life, by his choice, and he had chosen to let me go long before his death.

At the end of his life, his wife informed me he had cancer and it was progressing quickly. I asked them to visit since we still lived in the same town together. My father did come visit a couple of times after I spoke with my stepmother about his condition. I found out at that point that the cancer had started in his brain but had already spread to his lungs, liver and other organs. There was nothing left to do but make him comfortable until the end.

He seemed normal on the first visit. We really didn't spend much time talking to each other. My children and grandchildren were there and it was really just a relaxed visit with most of the attention on the kids. However, the second and last visit was much different. We were all visiting in the kitchen when I asked where dad had gone. He was by himself in the backyard looking for a four-leaf clover. He returned with one, and I found that very strange behavior for a grown man, and it got worse from there. I made lunch for us and while fixing our plates, I offered my father a sandwich. He refused and instead picked up a piece of bologna and sat down on the kitchen floor. He laid the meat on the floor for a few minutes and then picked it up and ate it. I was in shock.

By this time my stepmother said she wasn't getting much sleep because my father was getting up at all hours in the night. He was throwing things away and doing things that made no sense, though in his mind he was doing what needed to be done I guess. I remember feeling sadness for him at this point. Don't get me wrong, I don't have a cold heart in the least but I also have never been a pretender. I haven't ever been one who could fake emotions and this time was no exception.

He was distant, a stranger to me. It was then at the end I truly saw the real man. I went and picked him up so we could have lunch together. I was giving the chance for him to set things right with me. At lunch he told me about how proud and wonderful his other children were doing. He told me about their jobs, homes and children. I wondered what he would say about me. He never asked about me, my life or my future.

After lunch he wanted to visit old friends and look at their antique cars. When he introduced me, I was not his but my mother's daughter. He wanted to stop to get his other daughter her favorite dessert to take home and we did. He died not knowing what my favorite dessert is. He talked a lot about my sister and me driving him to visit his other daughter. He was never really there with me in the moment; he was missing the opportunity with me.

My father never saw me as I sat across the table that day having lunch. I waited and waited, even as he was dying at the hospital. I went and waited for my father to see me sitting there, see the pain and hurt he caused. I waited for him to take my inner child's hand and make it all better. That moment never came. He died as he lived, never acknowledging me, my life, my struggles and my pain. As always, he took the easy way out.

I will never understand how people saw my father as good. They use words like good husband, good father, good friend, brother and man. To me he was the cause of such pain. Even after his death, I still feel that pain.

Before this project, I never thought I needed to grieve my father's death. But in writing these words, I see I need to walk through it to heal my heart.

\*

BROOKE NINNI MATTHEWS
Brooke was 38 when her mother JoAnne
died at age 57 from cardiac arrhythmia

My beloved mother struggled for a year with many health problems including diabetes before her passing. In October 2010, my mother's brother took her into the ER because he noticed her face drooping as they were sitting at her dining room table, she had suffered a stroke. I remember that night so vividly because I was having a birthday party for my daughter at the time my sister called to tell me.

The following month, on November 6, my mother once again had to go into the ER. This time she had spiked a 106 degree fever. She was admitted and put in isolation because they were afraid she was contagious. They did a biopsy on her lung days following her admittance and said my mom had what was called BOOP, a rare pneumonia that only one percent of the population gets. Mom stayed in the hospital for a while and lost a lot of mobile ability, so she was then moved to a rehabilitation nursing home until she gained back some strength. She came home for a few weeks and then was once again admitted back into the hospital for an infection on the bottom of her right foot, and then from there moved yet again into a rehabilitation nursing home. Mom then left the rehabilitation nursing home and stayed with some family members, but it got difficult to care for her, as her foot was getting worse. Mom then agreed to go back into the hospital for her foot, and it was determined that she would need to have her right foot amputated up to the knee.

On July 11, 2011, my mother had her right foot amputated up to her knee. She stayed in the hospital for a few days afterwards, and then was once again moved to a rehabilitation nursing home. On August 4, 2011, my mom had two toes on her left foot amputated and, on August 6, we celebrated her fifty-seventh birthday in the rehabilitation nursing home.

On August 9, my husband, our children, and I went to visit my mother, and I had asked her if anyone had seen her about fitting her for her prosthetic leg. She said that they didn't need to because she was going home. I asked who told her that she was going home. She replied, "I don't know who it was that told me I was going home, but that's what they told me." I went out to the nurse's station to ask who told her that, and the nurses told me nobody ordered discharge papers. We spent some time with my mother and then left to go home. That was the last time I saw my mother alive. Sadly, my mother was right. She was going home, but not the home I was thinking of. Rather, she went to her eternal home. On August 10, 2011, sometime around 5 a.m., just three days after her fifty-seventh birthday, my best friend and beloved mother lost her battle to diabetes and heart disease, just six months prior to losing my younger brother to homicide. When I look back on my mother's life, she was never a really healthy person, she always suffered from health problems, for heart disease runs in our family.

*

RUTH PAPALAS<br>Ruth was 41 when her father David<br>died at age 62 of a heart attack

When Mom called in February and said, "Your dad was complaining about chest pains. I'm at the hospital with him now." My head spun. My heart hurt. What? Why? Not my dad. This can't happen to him, it can't happen to us. Our whole family was just together for Christmas. Dad and Mom had just taken the grandchildren sledding a week or so before.

Mom and Dad were married when they were seventeen and nineteen, and had me a year later. I had very young parents. My grandparents all lived until seventy-five and longer, so I KNEW my parents would be around for a long time.

I was forty-one-years-old. With the help of my friend and boss, we figured out I was too old and tired to continue to work at a restaurant. I was encouraged to go to school, get a degree and a new career. I knew that the old elementary school where I attended kindergarten, first, second, third, and sixth grade now housed a business college. My dad had taught at this same building for eighteen of his thirty-eight years of teaching. When I walked into that school to register, I could almost smell my past. It had been an elementary school, so the drinking fountains were short and the toilets were short. It made me smile. Since dad had been a basketball coach there for fifth and sixth grade, we spent a lot of time in the gym. The gym still had the same smell, even though it had been over twenty-five years since I stepped in there. I went to the office that Dad used when he substituted for the principal when the principal would take time off. The only smell missing was the cafeteria. Our favorite dish was the homemade apple crisp, which my dad loved. I learned how to make the apple crisp and took it to my dad. His compliment was, "It's almost as good as the school's."

When registering for classes, I was adamant about NOT taking speech class. However, it was a requirement so I took it the first quarter. One of our first assignments was an introduction speech. We were to introduce someone as if they were about to come in and speak. It could be anyone, famous, fictional, or real. I chose my dad. In my speech, I noted all of the above things about the school along with the fact that my dad was in his thirty-eighth year of teaching. I would like to present to you my dad, David Watkins. A week or so later, dad had the heart attack. The doctor said that a third of Dad's heart was dead. What does that mean? Will he be able to come home, to teach, coach and to fish?

Dad always attended the Sportsman's Show. He had planned to go in February, but now his heart was a third dead. My husband, in an effort to get him to the show, offered to take my dad in a wheelchair. All I could think was, "Dad would hate that!" I think I started grieving then. Just thinking about all the things my dad would be unable to do on his own, all the things he loved. He may be alive, but my dad was unable to care for his boat, fish, coach, teach, walk around the Sportsman's Show….it broke my heart. I worked myself up so much that I became short of breath. My mother-in-law rushed me to the hospital. Dad was in intensive care on oxygen, I was in the ER receiving a breathing treatment and oxygen.

My Dad had been working on a home for my brother. He had arranged to have a HVAC unit installed, which was installed while he was in the hospital. Mom was at the hospital telling dad that she thought they overpaid for the unit. Dad asked, "Is it in? Does it work? Let it go." Mom started to protest again. Dad repeated, "Is it in? Does it work? Let it go."

Dad was in the hospital for a week or so and then he was discharged home. He was on a restrictive diet. He was moving slower, but he was home. We went to dinner with Mom and Dad as was our Friday ritual. Dad had a cough, I was concerned. I didn't like that cough. On Saturday, I went to their house to get Mom to go to garage sales. Dad joined us, still with that cough. After a short time he agreed that we could stop at an urgent care. They sent us to the hospital. Dad was admitted. They wanted to keep him for observation. The nurses made him comfortable in a room and attached an oxygen tube and hooked him up to some other medical equipment including a heart rate machine. I'm not a nurse and don't know much about heart rates, but the machine Dad was hooked up to was reading 40. I stated my concerns to the nurse at the nurse's station. She told me not to worry. He's on the observation floor and everything was fine and assured me that they would take good care of him. When I left the hospital, we were told that we could pick Dad up Sunday after lunch.

I was sleeping and didn't hear the phone. My sister came to my house and woke me up. Dad had taken a turn for the worse. We went to the hospital. My mom, aunt and uncle were sitting at the end of his bed. Dad was gone. My sister and I were on each side of him. His face was still warm, but he was dead. I guess I screamed or something. I was out of my mind. The nurses and doctors came running. The doctor said, "I'm so sorry. He never complained. He never said anything was wrong. I'm so sorry." The nurse said that when she brought him something to eat just shortly before, Dad was joking with her.

My dad was a young sixty-two-years-old. He taught seventh grade, coached the seventh and eighth grade basketball team and ran up and down the court with the boys. He was coaching the team from his hospital bed. He was a charter fisherman. He worked on his boat, poles and fishing plugs. He worked around the house, played with the grandchildren, vacationed in Canada and Myrtle Beach. He was funny. Dad was active, especially in the church. He was a Christian. He never smoked or drank. How can this be?

The basketball team won the championship game wearing black armbands. The basketball team invited my mom and us kids to attend the basketball banquet where they awarded my mom the winning basketball signed by the team. The basketball team had a basketball of carnations sent to the funeral home. The whole team came to pay their respects. They closed the school so that the teachers and students could attend the funeral. Dad was featured in the school newspaper with, "Some people come into our lives and leave footprints on our hearts and we are never ever the same." My dad was loved and respected and I miss him terribly.

*

MARY POTTER KENYON
Mary was 26 when her father Byron died at age 61 following a fall
Mary was 51 when her mother Irma died at age 82 from lung cancer

I was twenty-six-years-old and pregnant with my third child when my father was found badly injured at the bottom of a stairwell. He died shortly after, and we never learned what had really happened to cause his fall. Years later, that lack of closure plagued my mother and she hired a private detective, but it was too late to discover the truth behind my father's death.

I was in the doctor's office with my mother the day she heard the words, "You have lung cancer." While the doctor had not used the word "terminal," the cancer had spread to my mother's brain and I think we both knew right then. Mom was strangely silent, and I wondered if I was going to have to repeat the terrible words. Then I heard her murmur, "I always wondered what it was going to be."

My mother was a consummate artist and her biggest worry, besides the children she was leaving behind, was that she wouldn't

27

be able to paint or do any artwork. "I have a few paintings left in me," she informed the oncologist, and so it was decided that my mother would undergo radiation to shrink the growths in her brain. She would live less than three months from the diagnosis. My siblings and I cared for her as she lay dying on a hospital bed in her home. She went gently into the night on the evening of my fifty-first birthday. At first, I resented that; losing my mother on my birthday, but I eventually came to see that she had left behind a great gift in the faith that had sustained her all her life.

I would need that faith; my five-year-old grandson was diagnosed with cancer a month after my mother's death. In the doctor's office with my daughter, after the pronouncement that Jacob had cancer, we heard a single "Ave Maria" overhead on the radio, my mother's favorite song. Jacob went through surgery, radiation and chemotherapy before being declared cancer-free. When his cancer returned a year later, my husband couldn't bear to think of what the little boy he loved so dearly would have to endure. My husband died of heart failure. Seventeen months later, eight-year-old Jacob died too.

My mother left behind a legacy of faith and creativity. It was because of the unpublished manuscripts she left behind that I decided to get serious about my hobby of writing. And it was because of her admonition to her children to "use their God-given talents" that I attended my first writer's conference. Four years later, I've had four books published and I teach workshops and do public speaking. I'm pretty sure my mother is smiling down on me.

*

MARY LEE ROBINSON
Mary Lee was 56 when her father Pat
died at age 82 of a massive cerebral hemorrhage

Dad died just as he would have wished. He passed quickly, with my mother by his side. I was living out of state at that time, but had spoken to my dad by phone a few days before his death.

When he died, things were very good between us and nothing was left unsaid. Our last words to one another were, "I love you." And we meant it.

I've lost a lot of people who were dear to me. Dad was one of the easiest losses, only because there was no unfinished business and because Dad arranged all the details so well. The lessons I took away from Dad's death were to never miss an opportunity to tell someone you care about that you do, and to tie up or keep all the business of your life neatly. It makes a great hurt a little easier to bear if you do, and both of those lessons diminish regrets.

My dad was a pretty remarkable example of how to live. He was also a pretty remarkable example of how to die.

*

PATTI SULLIVAN
Patti was 14 when her father Alfred
died at age 61 from a heart attack

Alfred was my dad's name. He was tall and handsome, and a sharp dresser. He loved his daughters dearly and called us his four queens. I was born last, in his retirement years. My dad would take me on long walks, let me help him with house projects, and we played catch and "super ball." We listened to Doc Jones on the radio at breakfast. Dad always made the best pancakes with sugar, butter and syrup. He could cook, sew, and build things in the house. He and my mother bought and sold sixteen houses in eighteen years, and each one had some sort of remodeling done to it.

My dad started as a shoe model in Brockton, Massachusetts, which was once the biggest shoe capital in the world. In later years Dad became a shoe designer. He served twice in the Navy in Okinawa, my mother said Dad wanted to bring home all of the children he had met there. He wrote my mother notes in secret code to tell his locations.

Dad met my mother at the shoe company in Brockton, though his success came in California as a designer. I remember many black and white photos of his work which are now in a shoe museum in Massachusetts. Dad loved to play poker and have a little Seagram's Seven whiskey to get a glow. He was respectful and respectable. He loved to take little trips to "get the stink off." We would go to so many wonderful little towns in Maine, Vermont, and New Hampshire. Being patriotic, dad would always find a parade in those small towns. He was born on a farm in Brockton to Polish immigrants, and shared stories of his childhood. He loved life. He always said to us, "Stop and smell the roses." He loved his daughters and angered my mother by waking us when he came home from a long day at work. He was dedicated to his family.

Dad developed angina and underwent many heart operations. He was one of the first ten patients to have a vein transferred from the leg to the heart. He was able to watch that operation. He was the only one of the ten that lived. Dad took fifty pills a day including nitroglycerin.

When I was fourteen, my dad had undergone surgery at Massachusetts General Hospital. His roommate said Dad had taken a shower, stepped out of the stall with a smile on his face, and died. I had visited him and talked to him just the night before. That was the day my music died.

\*

JUDY TAYLOR
Judy was 55 when her mum Shirley
died at age 78 from a stroke

My mum....how do I write about my mum? I'm not sure I can put it into words right now. She was, like most human beings, a woman of many complexities. I too am a woman of many complexities so I guess we were similar in many ways. It feels to me we experienced every feeling and emotion I know in our mother-daughter relationship. At times we radiated together. At other times we were poles apart. I would have to say that the extremes in our experiences strengthened our relationship though it wasn't always easy. I feel, by the end of her physical life, we celebrated each other as a whole person; our best and worst.

Oh, how I would love her here physically to continue this relationship. However, that is not to be so I am delighted to say our ongoing relationship since her death has resulted from my commitment to writing to her and talking to her in spirit just as we did in life.

Mum died following a massive stroke just before midnight on February 5, 2011. We were dancing just moments before. Mum left the dance floor and collapsed. An ambulance was called and a journey began to the Alfred Hospital in Melbourne. Mum had an operation and, after two weeks in the intensive care unit, family and doctors agreed to remove her life support on February 20, 2011. She stopped breathing four hours later.

I can feel the emotion as I write. From my perspective, mum left her physical body the day of her stroke and patiently waited for everyone to accept the human reality of death. So for me she died on February 5, 2011.

I began feeling Mum's presence everywhere from that moment on, and whenever I was open to this reality she was there waiting for me. Over the coming days, weeks, months and years my writing became one of our most powerful connections. I set the intention to spend time with Mum by sitting on the front porch having a cup of tea, visiting places we loved together, going for walks, sitting in silence and lighting a candle, and many more things that resonated for us. At these times, I chatted with her just as we had in life. Our experience and connection was profound.

There were times in the early, days, weeks, months and years where the physical loss was so raw and unbearable that I could not feel her presence and I sobbed for my mummy. I just wanted my mummy back and nothing else mattered. The ache was unbearable and I believed I would never get over her loss.

And then she was there waiting for me, waiting for me to experience this human experience called grief in all its complexities. When I was ready, she let me know she was still here right beside me, waiting for me to experience this new relationship.

It is different now and it is truly beautiful. Our love has expanded beyond all boundaries and in many ways is stronger than the relationship we shared here on earth together. I am eternally grateful that she gave birth to me and shared this existence with the joys and frailties of being human. I am eternally grateful that she has shown me there is life beyond death.

*

ALEXIS VON UTTER
Alexis was 12 when her father Marc
died at age 57 from lung cancer complications

My dad was the main caretaker at my home. He drove me everywhere, taught me how to play the sports I do now, taught me all of the homework, helped me with my art and school projects, and taught me how to cook simple things. My dad was everyone's favorite person. He was kind, funny, an amazing cook, and smart. He was the best person to be around because he was happy. Everyone loved coming over to spend time with him and hear his jokes, along with a little salsa and guacamole on the side.

In May 2011, my dad had to have shoulder surgery. As he started healing in late August, his lower back started to hurt. It got to a point where he couldn't even get up by himself. My mom took him to the hospital and he wasn't getting much better, but they couldn't figure out what was wrong. My dad was flown over to Georgetown Hospital in Washington, D.C. We went to visit dad and found out he had stage four lung cancer. Dad had a respirator in his throat and couldn't talk. My mom had taken time off of work, but my brother just acted like nothing was really happening. I was falling apart, but my dad was staying strong.

On December 4, 2011, I had to say goodbye. Dad hadn't been able to move and he was blown up from the medicine. I later found out that a natural antibody designed to attack the cancer was instead attacking Dad's nervous system. There was nothing anyone could do. I had to say goodbye to my best friend and my dad. My dad was strong and let out few tears but he kept going for my family. At around 7:10 p.m., they took Dad off the life support and let him fall asleep. At 7:20 p.m., my father passed away.

My mom had to become two people and take care of us. I have had to have a nanny ever since. That day ruined my life but also helped me to learn so much more. To this day I can remember all the good times. But I will also never forget the horrible sadness on my dad's face when he realized he had to say goodbye.

*

HEATHER WALLACE-REY
Heather was 40 when her father John
died suddenly at age 71 of a massive heart attack

Since the day I was born, I was partially raised (my mom helped a whole lot!) by John Wallace: a father-teacher-turned bus driver-turned bus company owner who loved to read, loved great conversations, and adored his six children and fourteen grandchildren. My dad had a passion for life and wanted to share the things he was interested in with anyone willing to listen.

In April 2012, my dad was stolen from us. My father, probably one of the most physically fit seventy-one-year-old men you would ever meet, who spent his time running, biking, and going to the dojo, suffered a massive heart attack and passed away.

My dad died the same way he lived: on his own terms. At about 6:30 a.m. on the day he died, he told a man in his apartment complex that he wasn't feeling very well. Ten hours later, the pain was bad enough that my dad took the elevator down from his condo to the management office and asked the woman in the office to call an ambulance. She was the last person to have a conversation with him. My dad arrived at the hospital and, after numerous attempts to resuscitate him, we were told there was no hope. In a matter of four hours he had been rushed to the hospital, we had arrived at the hospital, he was there, he was gone, and we were on the way home with his personal affects, which included some random vials of ibuprofen, two sticks of lip balm, glasses, a Swiss army knife, a package of Kleenex, two keychains, a handheld game, a case with his hearing aid batteries, two books (one about tai chi), his sandals and socks, and a Shotokan karate jacket. I felt as if I was lovingly carrying the final possessions of MacGyver. Far be it for my dad to either wear his sandals without socks OR to not come prepared to a heart attack. This wonderful man who had taught us to "keep your winter gloves in the car, in case the car breaks down" and to "never let the gas tank get down to less than a quarter of a tank" was certainly not going to be caught unprepared.

Ironically enough, I know he certainly was not prepared for a heart attack at that moment, because he still had two unopened half gallons of "the good ice cream" in his freezer when he died. Those two half gallons would definitely have been opened and eaten if he had known he wasn't coming back for them.

CHAPTER TWO

# THE AFTERMATH

*Somehow, even in the worst of times, the tiniest fragments of good survive.*
*It was the grip in which one held those fragments that counted.*
MELINA MARCHETTA

Whether death is expected or not, in the wake of loss the first questions we ask ourselves are: How am I going to survive this? How can I function when I have no feeling or when my emotions are so strong they threaten to paralyze me? There we stand in the aftermath, feeling vulnerable and sometimes ravaged with fear. How do we survive?

*

SOPHIE BLOWERS
Sophie was 50 when her mother Amy
died at age 79 of internal bleeding

Immediately after mom died, I allowed myself to fall into my default, comfort mode. I am a bit of a control freak, and I had just lost control of my entire life as I had known it. I needed to control something just to make sure the world would not spin off its axis. I gravitated toward the things I felt I could control to create the illusion that I was not in a tailspin.

I had one sister and one brother with me, and we just began dividing tasks. If you have something to do, you don't have to acknowledge what just happened. Just get through the next task, check off one more box, do not think, do not let the enormity of what just happened touch you. Not yet. It was like sizing up an opponent in a boxing ring. I knew the fight was going to take place, but I had to dance around the ring a few times to determine how the battle would take place and where I needed to shield myself.

\*

CHRISTINE DUMINIAK
Christine was 57 when her mother Ann
died at age 86 from an abdominal aortic aneurysm

I survived the loss of my precious mother through fervent prayers to God, and the support of my two sisters and my husband. Sharing amusing stories about our mother really helped to change tears of sorrow into laughter.

\*

WENDY EVANS
Wendy was 14 when her father Dwight
died at age 32 in a plane crash

At age fourteen, I was old enough to understand that there was a lot wrong with what was going on after the funeral. Unfortunately I was not sophisticated enough to understand the cause of what was wrong. My mother was thirty-two-years-old at the time all this was happening. She lacked understanding of the financial piece of the will. Ultimately we were forced to move from our family home so it could be sold. My mother remarried and we had a completely different existence within about two months following the funeral. Adjustment was slow to happen. No one in our family saw our dad's body. His plane went down in the Everglades and the rescue took more than a day. His body was not in good condition for an open casket. Never seeing him dead, the three of us kids held on to hope for many years that he was still alive. I was stuck in the grief journey for nearly fifteen years without movement forward.

*

BONNIE FORSHEY
Bonnie was an infant when her father Andrew
died at age 41 from a cerebral hemorrhage
Bonnie was 60 when her mother Doris
died at age 81 from colon cancer

It was very hard to lose my mother. That is the first person who holds you, and loves you. You think she will always be there. When she died, it left a huge hole in my heart. Everywhere I go, there are memories of seeing her there, or taking her out to eat somewhere. She suffered from cancer. It took her independence and dignity from her. She was in great pain. She is free now. As much as it hurts me, I know that she is better off. I will see her again.

*

SKIP FRANKLIN
Skip was 41 when his mother Dianne
died at age 63 from a series of physical issues

My initial aftermath was one of guilt. I had been a little tough with my mom on the phone the night before. And in the morning, our discussion was still bothering me and so I left a nice voicemail message for my mom. And ended it by telling her that I love her. Later that same day, I found out she had passed. And my first response was, "When? When exactly did she pass?" I was hoping it was after my apology voicemail that morning. It meant a lot to know she heard my message. Their answering machine would broadcast messages across the bedroom, and I knew she passed in that room. So she would have heard the message.

To my great relief, my mom had passed several hours after that message. Knowing that she most likely heard it helped me cope.

37

*

KIMBERLY HAWKS
Kimberly was 9 when her father Charles
died at age 32 in a car accident

I can't say that I know how I survived the original aftermath. I was a young child when my father was killed. The moments shortly after his passing still feel like a daydream. I remember the feeling of having to be strong. My mother, brothers and sister were also scared, and I felt like I was the one who needed to be strong for everyone else. Perhaps I survived by burying my emotions behind a façade of strength.

*

VICKI HECKROTH
Vicki was 5 when her mother Bonnie
died at age 27 in an auto accident

I was too young to understand. All I really knew was my mommy was gone and wasn't coming back. I remember that there were people everywhere and they were all crying a lot. I spent much of my time clinging to my father, worrying that he would also go away and not come back.

*

TERESA HERRING
Teresa was 47 when her father Burton
died at age 65 from brain cancer

The day I found out my father passed is such a blur. It was a painful day for me but not for the obvious reason. My father was dying of cancer and in the last stages when he passed. About a week before he passed I received a text message from my stepmother saying that my father was going to hospice care. I worked in the medical field and knew that was the end of life care. I knew you did not come home from there and they were just making my dad comfortable until he passed. At the time I was still hurting about our last day together and I chose not to go visit him there. My last visit to the cancer hospital with him was painful for me. It really was a love fest for him and my sister, calling her over to sit next to him. I might as well not even been there. That visit did not end well either. My father called my husband into the room and kicked everyone else out, and gave my husband an hour-long speech about how to be a good man and he needed to man up. I found that appalling coming from the worst father ever, the man who never showed up when things were hard. My father chose to spend that hour with my husband and not me.

My father actually died the day before I found out he passed. No one called to let me know. The day I found out, I had sent a text to my sister, who was in from Georgia visiting my father, to see when she was going home. The response I received I will never forget. It read, "I will be staying until after the funeral." That was it. There in writing, I had been notified my father had died. Not one person thought to call me even though he had been dead for at least 24 hours at that point. Had I not texted my sister to see when she was going home, I don't think I would have been told of his passing. When questioned why I wasn't called, each one said, "Oh, I thought someone else called you." I was most hurt from my sister and I let her know it. I questioned why she didn't call me, why it never crossed her mind since I told her to let me know how my father was when she saw him. I was hurt she didn't think about me at all those two days. She would have been the first call I made. To this day, she or my family has never apologized for not calling me. My aunt's response was, "Why don't you grow up and take responsibility for your own actions?" This made me laugh. No one calls me and I need to take responsibility for my actions. All the while each of them is passing the responsibility off on each other.

For the first few weeks after finding out, I was just trying to gently deal with my own emotions. For the above reasons, I was dealing with my emotions alone. The emotions ranged from grief to anger, and everything in between. For instance I felt relief and happiness, all of which I thought was strange, and I was very confused by these and some other emotions too. I don't think I cried for the loss, but I do know I cried from the way my family both informed me of the death and the instant treatment after. I did a lot of searching for answers and trying to understand why I lacked emotions from my father's death, and why such strange emotions were present at the time. At first I wasn't even sure I cared that he died. I know that sounds harsh but to me it was kind of a relief. I didn't at the time understand that feeling.

*

BROOKE NINNI MATTHEWS
Brooke was 38 when her mother JoAnne
died at age 57 from cardiac arrhythmia

I think I handled my mother's passing well in the beginning. At the time I received the news of my mother's passing, I think I was more concerned with my brother and sisters. My husband lost his mother four weeks after I lost mine and, in all honesty, I don't think I had time to grieve the loss of my mother before his mother passed. And then, my only brother was murdered just six months later.

*

RUTH PAPALAS
Ruth was 41 when her father David
died at age 62 of a heart attack

I honestly have no idea how I got through losing my dad. My heart actually ached. My poor husband didn't know what to do with or for me. I was inconsolable. I remember having to wait a couple of days for the funeral as we waited for my brother to arrive. My brother had just driven to Key West and had to drive back home to South Carolina and then come to Ohio for the funeral. My aunts said they couldn't understand why it was my dad that died, and not them. They said they were old and had lived their lives. Why him? I did not really feel that way. I didn't want anyone to die. I remember a complete feeling of absolute loss.

\*

MARY POTTER KENYON
Mary was 26 when her father Byron died at age 61 following a fall
Mary was 51 when her mother Irma died at age 82 from lung cancer

I don't remember a lot about my father's unexpected death in 1986. It was a shock for the whole family, as he was found badly injured at the bottom of a stairwell and died in the hospital without ever waking up. I was pregnant with my third child and so busy with two young children. I do recall trying to protect them from seeing me cry. I wasn't seeing my mother daily or even weekly, so I'm afraid I wasn't much of a support system for her. I regret that deeply now, having lost a husband and intimately knowing the pain she must have gone through.

My mother remained alone for the next twenty-five-plus years. I was with her in the doctor's office when she was diagnosed with terminal lung cancer in August 2010. She died on my fifty-first birthday that November. We were all sideswiped by the deep grief we felt after her death. We were bereft. We were now orphans. A month after her death my five-year-old grandson was diagnosed with cancer, so that added to my grieving.

I spent many hours in my mother's house that winter; praying, writing and healing. I inherited many of her notebooks and took to heart the words she had written; that she wanted her children to utilize their God-given talents. Because of her words, I decided to take my writing seriously. I began working on a book and conducting workshops. I attended my first writer's conference and started working as a reporter for a local newspaper. I even designed a PowerPoint presentation for young mothers, encouraging them to utilize their creativity in their everyday lives. That PowerPoint consists of many slides showing what my mother accomplished as an artist while she was raising ten children in poverty. My mother was my artistic muse, and sometimes I feel her presence as I write.

*

MARY LEE ROBINSON
Mary Lee was 56 when her father Pat
died at age 82 of a massive cerebral hemorrhage

Like I do in all life crises, I function very well and fall apart later. I was devastated. My dad died, and my dad and I were very close. It was not really a shock, however, as he was 82 and his health had been failing. Dad was a big guy, six-foot five-inches tall, and he was used to being the one everybody leaned on. As he became elderly he developed some health problems, of course. Some of them meant that a wheelchair was looking like something that was going to have to be considered. Nobody would have been happy with that. Big men don't often enjoy being dependent on anyone. It makes them crotchety. Typically a very even tempered and happy guy might be rendered an unhappy camper when placed in a wheelchair.

Mom and Dad were planning on visiting my husband and I in West Virginia, from their home in Maryland. The visit was spurred by an event I was organizing at my church that my dad was especially excited to attend. We are Scottish, and I was chairing the committee for a Kirkin' O' the Tartan service, or a blessing of tartans that is traditional in many Presbyterian churches. I spoke to Dad on the phone the Wednesday before they planned to arrive. As we hung up, we both said, "I love you." It was the last time we spoke. The next day, Mom called to tell me that Dad suffered a massive cerebral hemorrhage, and was gone in two hours. I can't think of a more fitting way for Dad to expire. He died quickly, not suffering pain or indignity for very long. I'll bet it was the way he would have wished.

The service at my church was scheduled for two weeks away. My husband and I had time to make a quick trip to Maryland to be with my mom. She was adamant that we would make Dad's arrangements around the planned church service in West Virginia. Dad's memorial service could wait. Daddy would have agreed, wholeheartedly. That is exactly what we did. Dad was always my biggest cheerleader, encourager, reality checker and moral compass. Anyone who knew the two of us will tell you I was a daddy's girl. He's the person who challenged me to tackle new projects, stretch my talents, and reach higher. Dad had put together some local events, Scottish and otherwise, himself and was tickled pink that I was running with the baton. He didn't want to miss this show!

I returned to West Virginia in time to coordinate the event, with the help of other church members who stepped in to lend a hand. There was a lot of work to do, as there was a bagpipe parade down our main drag, a Scottish luncheon afterward, and press coverage, including TV, for all of it. I could not have completed everything without a whole lot of help from others. I also made sure that Dad was represented in spirit, if he couldn't be there in body. I wore my own kilt in his family tartan, but I added his tartan fly, the massive shoulder sash in the same fabric. Normally only worn by the men, it was a lot of material, but I think he would have been happy about that too. The Kirkin' O' the Tartan came off without a hitch, and my husband and I went home and called Mom. It was a pretty bittersweet moment.

\*

PATTI SULLIVAN
Patti was 14 when her father Alfred
died at age 61 from a heart attack

A foggy haze. I remember the day the principal came to give me a ride home, so I knew something was up. I had just talked to Dad the night before. He was my buddy. At that point in time, my dad was both parents. I cried on him when I got my period. He spoiled me. He hemmed my dresses.

I remember the funeral home. My sister took me for an ice cream. My mom, in her mental state, was drugged. Soon after my dad's death we took a trip. I remember my mom had some newfound freedom. She had many wigs: blonde, red, brown, long, cropped. I watched the transformation.

\*

JUDY TAYLOR
Judy was 55 when her mum Shirley
died at age 78 from a stroke

The first days, weeks, and months were like a rollercoaster ride. It was numb, raw with mixed emotions, tears, laughter and more. Feelings and emotions took me completely by surprise. I sat in bed most nights with my Mum's shawl wrapped around my shoulders in silence. Sometimes I could feel her presence. Sometimes I ached for her. In the first six months I did not pick up a book once. I love reading so this was unusual for me. At times I felt I accepted my new reality. At other times I resisted the reality that Mum was never going to walk up the pathway again. When I embraced my feelings and let them flow, healing began and I could feel her presence everywhere. When I resisted my feelings, the pain manifested in my body with severe back pain and illness from a weakened immune system. Surrendering to whatever presented supported me.

\*

ALEXIS VON UTTER
Alexis was 12 when her father Marc
died at age 57 from lung cancer complications

I just tried staying to myself and being alone, that is what helped the most. I had to be alone because I couldn't comprehend what was going on, and everyone bringing it up was too much for me.

\*

HEATHER WALLACE-REY
Heather was 40 when her father John
died suddenly at age 71 of a massive heart attack

In the blur of the days and weeks after my father's death, I had an onset of what I will refer to as "a gap" in my personality that included things I would never in a million years have previously done, including joyriding in my lingerie and being pulled over by the police, watching a fourteen-hour marathon of the reality TV show *Bridezillas*, refusing to get out of my favorite pink sweatpants for almost two weeks until my husband drew a line in the sand on that one, and refusing to eat ice cream and other foods my father and I used to mutually enjoy. I also had dramatic crying episodes, one in an elevator full of complete strangers, and yet again in the parking lot of Best Buy. I needed to be wearing a neon yellow warning label that read: Last hysterical crying episode = zero days. I know that grief counselors often disagree on the stages of grief, but given the chance to write my own stages, the beginning stage for me was what I would refer to as, "The crazy gremlin that I didn't recognize in the mirror who did things the real me would never have previously done." I have read that grief sometimes magnifies the worst qualities in the person that is grieving. In my case, you could have been standing on Mars and still have been able to see how erratic my behavior was. When people ask, "How did you cope with all of this?" I have only two answers, the first being that my cousin, who lost her dad a year earlier, told me, "It doesn't get better, it gets less awful." I have clung to her words since, and they still serve me well today. It DOES get less awful. My second answer is that the people who love me really, really loved me through the most difficult time of my life. I owe every moment of coping to my husband, my children, my best friend, my closest friends who had "been there," my most compassionate friends who told me I could call them, even in the middle of the night and the three hundred or so people who brought our family lasagna (church families really like lasagna) so I never had to cook.

*In every conceivable manner,*
*the family is link to our past, bridge to our future.*
ALEX HALEY

\*

CHAPTER THREE

# THE FUNERAL

*Some are bound to die young.*
*By dying young a person stays young in people's memory.*
*If he burns brightly before he dies, his brightness shines for all time.*
UNKNOWN

For many the funeral represents the end while for others it marks the beginning of something eternal. Regardless of whether we mourn the absence of our parent's physical body or celebrate the spirit that continues on, planning the funeral or memorial service presents emotionally-laden challenges shared by many.

*

SOPHIE BLOWERS
Sophie was 50 when her mother Amy
died at age 79 of internal bleeding

We actually delegated much of the funeral planning to the grandchildren. Both of my sons are pastors and one of my nieces is a dream at planning events. My sons planned and conducted the service, while my niece planned the reception afterward. It was a special time that allowed Mom's children to breathe and grieve and teach the next generation to take ownership and pay homage to their ancestors. I look back with incredible pride, as I think how

Mom raised us and we, in turn, raised our children to carry on our family's heritage with honor. That day was a way of saying, "Well done, Mom, well done."

*

## CHRISTINE DUMINIAK
Christine was 57 when her mother Ann
died at age 86 from an abdominal aortic aneurysm

My two sisters and I planned the funeral services together. We chose the same undertaker that my mother used for our dad's funeral. We liked and trusted them, and they felt like family. They were very kind and helpful in gently guiding us. We had a traditional Catholic viewing, mass and cemetery burial all on the same day. My mother had already shown us the dress she wanted to wear for her viewing, a year before she passed. My sisters and I were in agreement about everything. We were able to choose all but one hymn for my mother's funeral mass, because we were at a loss over how to pick the final one. The very next day after meeting with the funeral home owner, I was lying in bed and heard a hymn that I was unfamiliar with playing over and over in my head. It was, "Loving and Forgiving Are You, Oh Lord." I realized that my mother was there in the room with me and was letting me know she wanted this particular hymn played at her funeral. I was elated that she not only was aware of our dilemma, but that she came from Heaven to help with her funeral preparations. But I also realized that my mother was sharing with me that she personally found out just how loving and forgiving the Lord was.

*

## WENDY EVANS
Wendy was 14 when her father Dwight
died at age 32 in a plane crash

My father's twenty-four-year-old wife of twenty-eight days planned the funeral. My experience was profoundly difficult. I did not have much of a coach to understand what was happening. My mother was bewildered too. The funeral was eventful. My dad's adopted mother and aunts intended to open the closed casket during the viewing so they could see the body. It was loud and uncomfortable due to the circumstances. There was nothing helpful about the memorial.

\*

BONNIE FORSHEY
Bonnie was an infant when her father Andrew
died at age 41 from a cerebral hemorrhage
Bonnie was 60 when her mother Doris
died at age 81 from colon cancer

My mother planned her own funeral. She had it prepaid, bought her own nightgown, flowers, etc. She didn't want to be a burden on anyone. She was very brave and didn't want to add any more stress to her family.

\*

SKIP FRANKLIN
Skip was 41 when his mother Dianne
died at age 63 from a series of physical issues

We held a memorial service in November, over a month after mom passed. And it was wonderful. I got to see many of my parents' friends whom I had not seen for a long time. Great stories were shared and tears were shed. But it took place so long afterward, it really was not part of the emotional equation for me as far as handling her passing.

\*

KIMBERLY HAWKS
Kimberly was 9 when her father Charles
died at age 32 in a car accident

My mother and family planned the funeral. I remember watching my brothers and sisters, and giving them support. I remember climbing into bed with my mom and holding her while she cried. The day of the funeral I remember the pastor who gave the sermon presented each one of us children with a teddy bear. I don't even remember crying then. It was a small funeral home on the outside of town. I had been there the year before when my great-grandmother passed, and I remember thinking how weird it was that my daddy was the one in the casket this time. I remember there being ham and cheese sandwiches and my little sister trying to sneak off with all the mints. Strangers and members of the family that I had never met kept coming up to me and giving me a hug and tell me how sorry they were. I remember thinking to myself, "Why did it take my dad dying for you to finally meet me?"

I remember that there were yellow roses and purple flowers everywhere. My father really liked yellow roses. He always wanted to go to Texas, and he told me that the yellow rose was the flower of Texas.

They had an open casket though a lot of the family protested. My dad's body was really damaged in the car accident and many people felt that he should not be seen in that condition. I remember my mom asking me what I thought about the casket being open and I felt that it would be important for us children to see my dad one last time so we could say goodbye. But when I walked up to the casket and looked at my dad, he wasn't there anymore and I think for the first time in my life I realized how mortal we were. That was a hard lesson to learn at the age of nine.

*

VICKI HECKROTH
Vicki was 5 when her mother Bonnie
died at age 27 in an auto accident

My father and grandparents planned the funeral. I remember the Catholic priest saying to us kids that my mom was sleeping. For a five-year-old, this was traumatic. I couldn't understand why she didn't just wake up, and why we would have to put her in that box in the ground just because she was sleeping. I had awful dreams of them doing the same to me if I went to sleep.

We had always attended church on Sundays, but after my mom's death my father blamed God and we stopped going.

*

TERESA HERRING
Teresa was 47 when her father Burton
died at age 65 from brain cancer

My father was diagnosed with terminal brain cancer and survived for several months which allowed him to prepare for his funeral. As far as I know the funeral was planned by my father, his wife and their children. I think maybe my sister also helped, but I never asked. Perhaps I helped in a roundabout way, because on the day of the last time I spent with my father he wanted to go speak to the funeral director about something. I didn't go in or ask what it was about. I secretly hoped he was changing things to make everyone mad. I was hurt that we were wasting time on this stuff when he and his wife should have handled this and probably already did. I was angry we were spending the last day we would have together doing chores.

When he passed, I was still angry with him for wasting so much time or perhaps for not doing what I needed him to do, which was help me to heal. When I found out he had passed, I spent a lot of time looking at the situation and asking myself questions about how I was going to mourn the loss. I spoke with my husband and told him not to give his opinions on what he felt I should do because I wanted to process and decide for myself what I could live with when it was all over. I wanted no influence.

After deciding what was right for me and my mourning process, I spoke with my sister and before I told her about the decisions I had made, I wanted us to make an agreement that no matter how we handled the upcoming events, we would not judge each other and would respect what we chose to do or not do. To me that was important because I knew my sister and I had two very different experiences with our father, both as children and adults. At the time she was the only relationship in this scenario that I tried to keep intact; the others were never really healthy relationships anyway.

I spent hours asking myself if I would regret not going to the service. Would I regret not going to my father's home? Would I regret not saying goodbye, seeing him one last time? Would I regret not going to the funeral? I really wanted to take care of myself and not just do what was expected of me. Clearly my father never did what I expected him to do either. For me the answer to all the questions was no. I would be fine if I chose to not make the effort to do these things. I was just never one to fake emotions. I didn't want to go and pretend that my father was a good man, that I forgave him for not being the father I needed, or that these were the people who I really cared about. I didn't want to comfort or be comforted by any of them. In fact, each had played a part in the pain from my childhood. Whether it was an active or passive role, each of them knew what happened, and none of them tried to prevent it. I was not ready to just pretend that didn't matter for the sake of burying my father. My absence at the funeral spoke very clear how I felt.

I did choose to go to the gravesite a few weeks later and took some Dollar Store flowers. I say it that way because I remember going to get the flowers and just wanting the cheapest ones I could find, and saying to myself that my father wasn't worth anything more. He didn't have a headstone placed yet, but I found his grave and just spent a few minutes with him there. I cried and asked why didn't he love me, why didn't he care? I got the same answers I would have got if he were alive: None.

To this day, I don't regret how I chose to handle my father's death, funeral and family. I don't feel any guilt from not being a fake person and doing what was expected of me. I think the relationships we have with each other are unique and, at the end of the day, we are the ones who have to take a look inside and make the right choice for ourselves. And that choice may not always line up with what others think is best. Your true family and friends will understand. They will look at the whole picture and support you even if they can't fully understand the entire situation. They can and will support and believe that you are doing what is right for you.

*

BROOKE NINNI MATTHEWS
Brooke was 38 when her mother JoAnne
died at age 57 from cardiac arrhythmia

My husband, my sisters and I had my mother cremated and her ashes divided among us. We had a memorial for her at a church our aunt belonged to at the time.

*

RUTH PAPALAS
Ruth was 41 when her father David
died at age 62 of a heart attack

Mom did most of the funeral planning. She seemed to be the only one of us under control, which is something I still can't comprehend. We went to the funeral home with her. I remember thinking, "I didn't even know there were this many choices (casket sizes, shapes, colors and wood) to make." I know I cried the whole time. How do you pick the perfect casket for someone? How can there be such a thing? I was just not mentally or emotionally prepared for losing my dad.

My dad was the seventh grade basketball coach. When we walked into the funeral home and there was a carnation wreath made to look like a basketball near the casket from his basketball team, I didn't know whether to smile or cry. When the entire basketball team and the other coaches came through the funeral home line, I cried.

When Mom planned the funeral bulletin, she had the verse, "*I will make you fishers of men,*" (Matthews 4:19) on the front of the funeral bulletin. Dad was a fisherman who ministered by taking pastors on fishing excursions. One of my dad's fishing buddies, Rev. Fred Blauser, was also the pastor of the church and performed the funeral ceremony. I was asked to share a memory during the service. I wrote it out because I have a hard time speaking in front of large groups of people. Once I started reading aloud about camping and fishing in Canada and our memories there, I began sobbing. Pastor Fred finished reading for me. The realization that none of that would ever occur hit me really hard.

One of the songs sung at my dad's funeral was, "It Is Well with My Soul." To this day, when that song is sung at church, I can't sing along to all of it, because it still takes my breath away and there is a huge lump in my throat.

Dad was a Sunday school teacher, the Sunday school bus driver and also played basketball with the guys from church. Another very memorable song from my dad's funeral was by Ray Boltz, titled simply, "Thank you." The song lyrics are beautiful and remind me so much of my dad.

## THANK YOU

*I dreamed I went to heaven, and you were there with me*
*We walked upon the streets of gold, beside the crystal sea*
*We heard these angels singing, then someone called your name*
*You turned and saw this young man, and he was smiling as he came*
*And he said friend you may not know me now, and then he said, but wait*
*You used to teach my Sunday School when I was only eight*
*And every week you would say a prayer before the class would start*
*And one day when you said that prayer*
*I asked Jesus in my heart*

## CHORUS

*Thank you for giving to the Lord*
*I am a life that was changed*
*Thank you for giving to the Lord*
*I am so glad you gave*
*And said remember the time*
*A missionary came to your church*
*And his pictures made you cry*
*You didn't have much money*
*But you gave it anyway*
*Jesus took the gift you gave*
*And that's why I'm here today*

*One by one they came, far as your eyes could see*
*Each life somehow touched by your generosity*
*Little things that you had done, sacrifices you made*
*They were unnoticed on the earth, in heaven now proclaimed*

*And I know that up in heaven, you're not supposed to cry*
*But I am almost sure, there were tears in your eyes*
*As Jesus took your hand and you stood before the Lord*
*He said, my child look around you, for great is your reward*
*I am so glad you gave.*

My dad was supposed to retire. My brother was going to send Mom and Dad on a cruise for his retirement. Instead, my brother paid for the tombstone and then for Mom to join my brother's family on a cruise. My mom's name was engraved on the tombstone. Dad died in 1998. Mom allowed them to engrave her birthdate, but they were not allowed to put 19--. She planned to live into 2000. She's still with us. I was very grateful to my brother for what he did for Mom.

*

MARY LEE ROBINSON<br>
Mary Lee was 56 when her father Pat<br>
died at age 82 of a massive cerebral hemorrhage

The real answer to that question is Dad planned the funeral. My folks were both pretty grounded-in-reality kind of people. Mom is a retired nurse practitioner. She did some private duty nursing in the days before hospice care. My dad was a combat veteran who served in two theaters of war. He was also a retired property manager of a residence for seniors. In short, they were both acquainted with death. It was discussed in our home when I was growing up, as the natural part of life that it is.

My husband and I met and married in our early fifties. Both of us had lost grandparents as well as aunts and uncles. We had also buried my husband's father. We too, were pretty realistic about the cycle of life. Because of that, I had requested both my parents to give some thought to their last wishes, and give me some kind of guidance. I didn't need to know it before I needed it, but I wanted some idea on how to honor my parents in the way that they wanted.

Dad let me know that he had done as I asked and showed me where he kept the three-ring binder with his notes. I don't recall that we reviewed it, but I think he told me the topics that he had addressed. With that task completed, I didn't give it much more thought. I knew in general terms that my dad wanted to donate his body to the Board of Anatomy for science research, and that they would return his cremains to us after one year. He had been an active community volunteer for decades, and he wanted to continue to serve. It seemed perfectly apropos. Upon his death, Mom and I retrieved the notebook and started going through it. There was a great deal of thought put into it. Dad had all of his financial records organized in one section. Possessions of value or significance were cataloged. Dad had listed some of his favorite scriptures and hymns, and he asked that I deliver his eulogy. Gulp. That was a tall order! Dad requested that we arrange for a single bagpiper to play at his service, and gave me four or five names and phone numbers to contact. He did not write his obituary, but he listed in bullet points all of the relevant facts of his life so that I could write it.

As his cremains were not going to be available for a while, he requested a memorial service followed by a Celtic Wake or, in other words, a giant party, and he gave us several options for his ashes. None of those have been done. Eight years later, Mom's not ready. Dad is still in the bottom of her closet.

Because Dad was to be memorialized rather than buried in a casket, we were able to plan the service for about three weeks out, a week after the Kirkin'. The church where Mom and Dad belonged was not available for the date that we needed, so the service was conducted in the auditorium of the senior campus living building where they lived. We expected good friends and a few neighbors would attend. Mom and I were stunned when people started arriving. They just kept coming! We dispatched my husband to direct traffic in the parking lot. We pressed a family friend into service in the lobby to point guests to the auditorium. All kinds of people came from the many organizations where Dad had volunteered including Boy Scouts of America, church, Jaycees, the hospital, American Legion, Fort McHenry, all over. A National Park officer from Ft. McHenry pulled me aside and told me that he had lost count at 250 people, and he counted crowds for a living.

The service began a little late, as the staff scrambled to find more chairs. Once it began, there was another surprise. I asked one of the bagpipers on the list to come and play. He did. He also brought all the other members of the bagpipe band that Dad used to lead as drum major. There were twelve bagpipers in all, and they piped Mom and me to our seats. I delivered Dad's eulogy and managed to get through it without crying. Three different organizations presented Mom and I with American flags and one Bible. Then we adjourned to the American Legion for lunch. About one hundred and fifty people attended that. People milled around, telling stories, sweet and funny. We still had one more surprise coming. Each of the twelve bagpipers mounted the stage and each gave a toast to my dad with single malt Scotch, his favorite. Celebration of a life well lived. Dad would have had a great time!

*

### PATTI SULLIVAN
Patti was 14 when her father Alfred
died at age 61 from a heart attack

I was fourteen. I remember the Mass cards being printed. I am sure my older sisters helped. I cried a lot. I remember kissing my dad's waxy face in the casket; my handsome daddy. I am sure I ate…coping skills.

*

### JUDY TAYLOR
Judy was 55 when her mum Shirley
died at age 78 from a stroke

My dad planned my mum's funeral with various contributions from the daughters. My mother had a wide circle of friends from the different passions she embraced in life. It was a beautiful celebration. My mother was cremated and her ashes buried a few months later when family members living overseas were able to attend. I personally would have liked to have had more involvement in the process.

*

ALEXIS VON UTTER
Alexis was 12 when her father Marc
died at age 57 from lung cancer complications

My mom mostly planned it with my brother and I, and a priest at our parish. I had to be strong, this was the first time I had seen my mom cry and I knew at that moment she needed me to hold her.

*

HEATHER WALLACE-REY
Heather was 40 when her father John
died suddenly at age 71 of a massive heart attack

Since my dad died suddenly, there was no advance planning on how his funeral should look. He had never discussed his wishes, except that his driver's license indicated that he wanted to be an organ donor. We had never discussed who would be Dad's next of kin. However, since I am the oldest and my parents were no longer together, I drew the short straw. Imagine my delight, and by delight, I mean, hideous panic attack when I thought I might ACTUALLY vomit when I found out I got to decide whether or not they should pull the plug. Lucky for me, my parents raised all five of my siblings and me to advocate a democratic form of government, so I was at least able to poll the other family members in the room that day, instead of making the decision on my own.

We had never discussed who would be the executor of my dad's estate, or anything about burial or cremation. We had never discussed what type of a memorial service would best represent my dad. In order to understand almost anything about my dad's funeral, you need to know two things about my family. First, we are nothing if not creative. Second, we are late for everything.

My dad, who was born a true Scotsman and raised as a Presbyterian, converted to Buddhism in the last three years of his life. My five siblings and I met and decided that no memorial

59

service for my dad would be complete without having each of these religions or traditions represented. We remained dedicated to keeping things interesting. My dad was cremated, the urn with his ashes draped with our Scottish clan's tartan.

Most of my siblings and I had responsibilities for my father's funeral. Mine was mostly to keep everyone organized. My younger brother, who was married and had two small children at the time, was responsible for picking up the urn with my dad's ashes at the crematorium and bringing "Dad" to the funeral.

I can remember telling my siblings what time they needed to be at the service, because I'm bossy like that. The day of the memorial service, my younger brother - we'll call him "the transporter"- was almost late for Dad's memorial service. I can remember being grief-stricken, but not so much that it kept me from being irritated: our family cannot be on time even for our father's funeral. My brother wasn't late for the funeral, he just wasn't fashionably early, as I had probably unreasonably demanded. He showed up minutes later, running like a quarterback with an urn under his arm with his wife and two baby girls in tow.

I took the "older sister" tone with him:

Me: Where WERE you?

Him: You really want to know?

Me: Yes. You were almost late. Where WERE you?

My brother and his family lived in a third story walk-up condo with an elevator, and the kids always wanted to take the elevator.

Him: Well, we were on the way down in the elevator when I realized that SOMEONE (pointing to my dad's urn with a hitchhiker's thumb gesture) hadn't spoken up and I had to go back and GET him.

And so, even when death is involved, I cannot be mad at my siblings because they make me laugh so hard.

The memorial service was held in the chapel of the Presbyterian home, an assisted living center where my grandmother lived. It was a traditional Presbyterian funeral complete with hymns and prayers and preaching. But it also had a Buddhist twist, complete with chanting, incense swirling and gong banging. Last but not least, my father's funeral began and ended with bagpipes, thanks to a woman who was known in certain circles as Bagpipe Mary.

When one begins to envision a lady bagpiper, I think of old musicals like *Brigadoon* or Disney movies like *Brave*, some sweet little redhead with a feisty temper, playing a bagpipe while wearing a kilt. Bagpipe Mary was wearing a kilt, alright. But instead of the feisty, sweet, curly-haired young girl from a quaint little town somewhere near Edinburgh that disappears into the mist each night, Bagpipe Mary looked like she had come straight out of the mist of East Compton. In other words, Bagpipe Mary was not someone you would want to meet in a dark alley. I'm pretty sure that not only could she play those bagpipes, but she probably also knew at least seventy-two ways to kill you with those bagpipes, if necessary. My dad would have loved Bagpipe Mary.

People told us it was the most unique memorial service they had ever attended. I think by unique they meant weird. My dad would have expected nothing less.

\*

*My mom taught me many things in life,*
*except how to get through life without her.*
BROOKE NINNI MATTHEWS

\*

CHAPTER FOUR

# THE TRANSITION

*The bereaved need more than just the space to grieve the loss.*
*They also need the space to grieve the transition.*
LYNDA CHELDELIN FELL

As we begin the transition of facing life without our parent, some find comfort by immediately returning to a familiar routine, while others find solitude a safe haven. Sometimes our circumstances don't allow choices to ponder, and we simply follow where the path leads. But the one commonality we're all faced with is the starting point that marks the transition from our old life to the new.

*

SOPHIE BLOWERS
Sophie was 50 when her mother Amy
died at age 79 of internal bleeding

I returned to school right away. I was in the last semester of my degree, taking nineteen credit hours and could not take time off or even stop to think. The good part was that I avoided any true grief. The bad part is that eventually grief catches up with you, and the reality of loss sinks in. Whether it comes as a slow memory or flash, or a crash like a tidal wave, it will happen. And it will hurt.

\*
### CHRISTINE DUMINIAK
Christine was 57 when her mother Ann
died at age 86 from an abdominal aortic aneurysm

My husband and children returned back to school and work right away, since the loss was not that life-changing for them, even though they were sad. In my particular case, I am an independent grief counselor and author, so I really didn't take a hiatus. However, I found that the support from those who I have counseled was very helpful to me in healing my painful heart.

\*
### WENDY EVANS
Wendy was 14 when her father Dwight
died at age 32 in a plane crash

As I recall my brothers and I went back to school after the week of the funeral. I was in my first year of high school. It felt like everyone knew what happened but nobody said anything to me. Very uncomfortable. It was a difficult transition. I am sad thinking of it now.

\*
### BONNIE FORSHEY
Bonnie was an infant when her father Andrew
died at age 41 from a cerebral hemorrhage
Bonnie was 60 when her mother Doris
died at age 81 from colon cancer

I am not working due to medical problems, but life without her has been difficult. I just have to try to block things out and keep going forward.

*

SKIP FRANKLIN
Skip was 41 when his mother Dianne
died at age 63 from a series of physical issues

I was in Seattle and my mom passed in southern California. And the distance both helped and hindered the process. I was involved in two demanding startup companies at the time, one as CEO and the other as Chairman. The immediate challenge I had to face was a complete loss of all ambition. I just quit caring about being successful. I just did not care. For someone like me, that was most strange. I remember thinking, "Why bother?" and saying to myself, "My mother is gone now, there is no longer a reason to be successful." My motivation factor had just left the building. This helped trigger a downward emotional spiral that included a lot of darkness. And my path out of that darkness I recounted earlier with my "Pillar of Light" moment.

*

KIMBERLY HAWKS
Kimberly was 9 when her father Charles
died at age 32 in a car accident

Everything after the funeral was a daze. I don't think we had much time before we returned to school. I was in the fourth grade and I remember feeling really lost. Everybody in my small town knew my family, as we were one of the founding families of the city. I remember a lot of kids whispering and talking at school. Some kids were nice and very helpful. Again, I remember being strong and not letting anyone see how much I was hurting. Some kids were really mean. I was part of the 4-H group and I remember one day we were all roller skating and some kids started teasing me and saying, "Too bad, so sad. Don't you wish you had a dad?" I don't think that people really ever stop to think about how words can hurt someone, and how some words can stay in your mind for life.

I got really lucky however. I was in fourth grade at the time and had a really good teacher named Miss Betty John. She was also the school principal. She took me in and gave me extra projects to keep me busy at school. She was more of a friend and a mother and a mentor to me than most people have been in my life. And I think if it wasn't for her, I would not be where I am today. Those people who come into your life when you are at your worst, and even the ones who come into your life when you are at your best, I truly believe are angels from God. My mother had a really hard time after the accident, and to deal with her grief she found herself in another relationship rather quickly. In a matter of twelve months my life changed completely. And up until two years ago, I never fully dealt with the death of my father.

\*

VICKI HECKROTH
Vicki was 5 when her mother Bonnie
died at age 27 in an auto accident

I went back to school two weeks later. There were lots of hugs, tears and cards from my classmates. I was in kindergarten at the time and I still have the cards and such. Every once in a while, I get them out to read. Because there was no such thing as counseling back then, I never grieved properly. Still to this day, fifty years later, I still struggle with this loss.

\*

TERESA HERRING
Teresa was 47 when her father Burton
died at age 65 from brain cancer

When my father passed, I didn't miss any work. I really did not talk much about it to coworkers either. They knew my father passed but unless they asked, I didn't bring it up. If anyone asked about it though, for some reason I felt obligated to say," we were not that close." I guess that made me feel better, because I felt emotionless and didn't understand why. I had seen others lose a parent and they were distraught, crying and trying to understand the loss. So on some level I felt guilty for the lack of emotions. They just weren't there for me, and I felt guilty and ashamed because of it.

\*

BROOKE NINNI MATTHEWS
Brooke was 38 when her mother JoAnne
died at age 57 from cardiac arrhythmia

I don't work, so I really did not have to worry about returning to work. I do believe school was a little difficult for my daughter, but my son had no problem with the transition.

\*

RUTH PAPALAS
Ruth was 41 when her father David
died at age 62 of a heart attack

Mom was placed on leave at work and then eventually she just retired. My brother had to go back to South Carolina a few days after the funeral, as he had a company to run. My sister also returned a few days later to Cleveland to her teaching job. My other brother and sister-in-law moved in with my mom for a short time, as they were in the process of relocating. My other sister was a stay-at-home mom and lived close to Mom. I went back to work the next week. I was the bookkeeper for a very busy twenty-four-hour restaurant, and payroll had to get done. I would go in the middle of the night at first since I couldn't sleep anyways. My manager and supervisor were very supportive and worked around me. The other employees were also very supportive.

I was attending Trumbull Business College when Dad died. Since I had missed two weeks of school already, I was just going to withdraw from school. I didn't think I could catch up. I didn't feel like going to school anymore. The school still reminded me of Dad.

The guidance counselor there, who was an acquaintance of my dad, assured me that the teachers would work with me and to not quit. With his and the other teachers' patience and encouragement, I graduated a two-year school in eighteen months.

*

MARY LEE ROBINSON
Mary Lee was 56 when her father Pat
died at age 82 of a massive cerebral hemorrhage

At the time, I was not working for a paycheck so I was able to stay in Maryland with my mom for about a week. She decided that she would like to come back to West Virginia with me for the visit that she and Dad were planning. As we returned to West Virginia, I was driving a brand new car, merely weeks old. About half way home, we were following a large truck carrying lumber. It came unbound and two two-by-four boards came hurling straight at us. Neither Mom nor I could believe the one that glanced off the windshield did not penetrate it. It was time for a rest stop and I needed to gather myself before driving again. I think Mom did too. When we returned to the car, a gentleman approached us and pointed out that one of my tires was completely flat. It had taken on a nail. He helped us with the spare tire and we got the car to a dealer for a replacement. It was amazingly quick and easy to get it repaired. Mom and I are both convinced that Dad had something to do with all that.

My church family was great about helping us keep everything on track for the special Kirkin' service. They were equally nice when I got back with Mom. They went out of their way to be kind to her. My husband, not accustomed to an active church life, went to my pastor and asked what could be done for Mom and me. He arranged for altar flowers on behalf of Dad, and a mention in the service as a surprise. I was very moved about the way people reached out to us.

\*

PATTI SULLIVAN
Patti was 14 when her father Alfred
died at age 61 from a heart attack

I don't remember. I feel life ended for me. My mother had her own issues. I think I mourned his loss for ten years. I was going to try out for cheerleading and softball but my support system died with my dad. I didn't have any self-esteem anyway, then...boom!! High school was a huge blur. Drugs helped. By senior year I was pregnant. No teaching career for me. No career at all. My family wasn't a family without my dad. My mom had boyfriends (which I thought was gross), and I found consolation in other things.

Life has been a struggle ever since. I wish my dad could have hung out longer. I needed his help. I always hope that I am like him in some small way. He loved children, and I do too. He was artistic, and I like to think I am too. He said, "Stop and smell the roses," so I always do. My dad wrote a book the summer before he died. It was called *A Young Boy Who Grew Up*. I have not read it. I have it on my desk......forty-three years later. Maybe it is time.


\*

JUDY TAYLOR
Judy was 55 when her mum Shirley
died at age 78 from a stroke

I was about to embrace a full-time contract two days after Mum had her stroke. I was apprehensive about taking on the project and they couldn't wait for me to commence, so they replaced me and I was relieved. This meant I could sit with Mum every day in the hospital and it gave me time to grieve. I returned to a casual fundraising position I had with a nonprofit organization where I was able to choose when I worked. This gave me the flexibility to go with the flow, which supported me no matter how I was feeling.

*

ALEXIS VON UTTER
Alexis was 12 when her father Marc
died at age 57 from lung cancer complications

I wanted to go back to school the day after, but my mom wouldn't let me. So I ended up going back two days after. It was weird because everyone already knew what had happened and actually looked at me weird. My principal announced that I would be out for a week, but I was only out for a day. So people questioned why I was there and why I looked so happy.

*

HEATHER WALLACE-REY
Heather was 40 when her father John
died suddenly at age 71 of a massive heart attack

Being that I have worked for a church for years, I had both the best and worst of all situations as far as returning to work. My father died the Tuesday before Easter. The Easter Sunday immediately after he died marked the first Easter Sunday since I was four years old that I did not attend any church service. I am not sure every person I know with strong faith can understand this, but church was the last place I wanted to be following my dad's death. I was unable to sit in the sanctuary of the church where I worked in the weeks after my father died. It is difficult to go back to working for God and God's people when you feel as if God has let you down.

I went back to work about a week after my father's death and, while I felt supported by the people who came to his visitation, and those who brought food, and sent cards and flowers, I was also subjected to many, many things that well-meaning Christians say who have not experienced a deep loss. People said things like, "Your faith will get you through," or "This must be God's plan," or "He's in heaven dancing with the angels." All of these things were particularly unhelpful, not only because I wasn't ready to hear

70

them, but because I don't particularly believe in a version of God that has a plan that includes as much suffering as the past three and a half years have included for my family. I know people's bodies give out, but I'm not sure that can always be construed as "God's plan." For someone who is grieving, I don't believe that telling them that the death of someone they loved and miss terribly is part of God's plan is very reassuring. I'm also certain that telling the bereaved that their loved one is in a better place is not okay. I don't care if it IS in heaven, dancing with the angels, it isn't what they need to hear. It definitely isn't what I needed to hear. I don't care where they thought my dad was. I wanted him back, standing next to us.

Maybe grief made me selfish but I strongly believe that losing someone you love occasionally entitles you to at least a little selfishness as you heal. In my case, the support that being a member of a Christian community (and a church employee) should have provided only made things worse. It felt like I was initially surrounded by people who cared more about using Christian lingo on me than actually just sitting quietly and holding my hand, or just letting me cry with them. I have learned that sometimes silence, listening, and handholding are the best answers.

*

*It's okay to cry.*
*Giving in to the tears is terrifying,*
*like freefalling to earth without a parachute.*
*But it's vital to our wellbeing as we process the deep anguish.*
LYNDA CHELDELIN FELL

\*

CHAPTER FIVE

# THE QUESTION

*Grievers use a very simple calendar.*
*Before and after.*
LYNDA CHELDELIN FELL

One day we have parents. The next, one or both are no longer living, leaving some of us an orphan. With the parent-child bond perhaps the most fundamental of all familial ties, what emotions come up when others inevitably ask about our parents?

\*

SOPHIE BLOWERS
Sophie was 50 when her mother Amy
died at age 79 of internal bleeding

I am very matter of fact about it. I want to get the subject out and away from me as quickly as possible. I choose to keep answers short and to the point. I do not want to relive those last days in the hospital.

\*

CHRISTINE DUMINIAK
Christine was 57 when her mother Ann
died at age 86 from an abdominal aortic aneurysm

I let them know that my parents have died. But if I feel that someone is spiritually open to the concept, I will let them know that I get afterlife signs from them. So in my mind, they are not "dead", but in a different place, which I call Heaven.

\*

WENDY EVANS
Wendy was 14 when her father Dwight
died at age 32 in a plane crash

After forty-plus years, I answer that my mother is doing well. Not a shock for people to learn that I lost my father. It was much more shocking when I was younger. I do not feel emotional when someone asks about my father at this stage. I can think of it as a time in my life that happened and it is no longer sad or bad.

\*

SKIP FRANKLIN
Skip was 41 when his mother Dianne
died at age 63 from a series of physical issues

In most cases I say, "I lost my mama a while ago, but my dad is still living and doing fine." Once in a while, if the person has recently lost a parent, it will lead into a deeper discussion. There will be that instant bond of two people who can relate to a similar experience. And the discussion goes on from there.

\*
DONNA GORE
Donna was 26 when her father Donald
died by homicide in 1980

Typically, I respond by saying, "He was murdered by a career criminal, in the commission of a robbery set up by a female accomplice. Due to his other crimes, it took six-and-a-half years to come to trial." Sometimes I also say, "He was shot five times in vital organs and left to die. Although he bravely tried to drive himself to a hospital and did not make it."

\*
KIMBERLY HAWKS
Kimberly was 9 when her father Charles
died at age 32 in a car accident

I usually tell people I lost my dad in a car accident when I was very young. And that will usually end the conversation. But once in a while it leads to a deeper conversation.

\*
VICKI HECKROTH
Vicki was 5 when her mother Bonnie
died at age 27 in an auto accident

I tell people that my dad and stepmom are doing great. I don't usually share about my mom's death unless I am asked directly. It is still very painful for me and, after all of these years, people do not understand how it can still bring tears. I had a wonderful stepmom, I cannot complain. However back then you didn't hear much about men raising children on their own. My mother passed away in November, my dad remarried in March, and my younger sister was born in September. We were told to call my dad's new wife "mom" right away. It was a whirlwind of things happening way too fast for the mind of a five-year-old.

\*

TERESA HERRING
Teresa was 47 when her father Burton
died at age 65 from brain cancer

When asked about my parent who has passed I say my father has passed. I really always felt like he was dead anyway, since he took such little interest in my life. In a strange way it is easier to answer now that he has passed then when he was alive. Saying he has passed is much easier than saying either I don't know how he is, or I have no relationship with him. Most of the time saying he has passed ends the questions.

\*

BROOKE NINNI MATTHEWS
Brooke was 38 when her mother JoAnne
died at age 57 from cardiac arrhythmia

I tell them my mother passed away in August 2011. My mother was my best friend and I miss her deeply, but I am at peace with her death because I know she went peacefully in her sleep.

\*

RUTH PAPALAS
Ruth was 41 when her father David
died at age 62 of a heart attack

Dad was very well known in the community and his death was also known. They closed the school where he taught so that the students and teachers could attend his funeral. Everyone sees Mom and us out and about, so no one really asks. When Dad died, I don't think Facebook even existed. Since Facebook, everyone can "see" how Mom is doing. We post Mom's pictures all the time. I answer quite simply. My dad died of a heart attack at sixty-two-years-old. The closer I get to sixty-two, the more I realize how young that really is.

\*

### MARY POTTER KENYON
Mary was 26 when her father Byron died at age 61 following a fall
Mary was 51 when her mother Irma died at age 82 from lung cancer

I can easily say, "Both my parents are dead," without crying, but I still feel sad. Occasionally I blurt out, "I'm an orphan," because despite being over the age of fifty, that is what it feels like.

\*

### MARY LEE ROBINSON
Mary Lee was 56 when her father Pat
died at age 82 of a massive cerebral hemorrhage

My dad was eighty-two when he died, and well known in the community. Most people knew, and I didn't get the question very often. New acquaintances will ask now and then, but nobody is surprised that he is my "late" father. I'm in that phase of life. Since his departure was well-marked and his life celebrated, I'm very comfortable talking about it. He was a great guy and a fantastic dad. I'm very fortunate that I had him with me as long as I did. No regrets. I miss him, of course, but I hear his lessons in my head all the time. It's like he never really left.

\*

### PATTI SULLIVAN
Patti was 14 when her father Alfred
died at age 61 from a heart attack

I tell them that both of my parents are deceased. I tell them that my dad died when I was fourteen. I tell them that I mourned for him for a good ten years. Sorry, I don't exactly know when my mom died. I am not a very good daughter.

\*

JUDY TAYLOR
Judy was 55 when her mum Shirley
died at age 78 from a stroke

I share openly and honestly about the death of my mum with others. It helps me to be true to myself and celebrate my mum and the journey we experienced in life. It also helps me and others when I share the grief following her death and the ways I have found to stay connected with her.

\*

ALEXIS VON UTTER
Alexis was 12 when her father Marc
died at age 57 from lung cancer complications

I say they are fine. A lot of people know that I only have my mom so they usually just ask about her. But if I don't know someone and they ask, I don't bring up what happened or that my dad has passed.

\*

HEATHER WALLACE-REY
Heather was 40 when her father John
died suddenly at age 71 of a massive heart attack

I am three and a half years past the death of my father so, at the very least, I have learned to control my emotions when people ask about him. It often comes up around his birthday, because he had a number of social media accounts, and Facebook in particular likes to remind everyone when it's his birthday. I can't bear to have his account taken down. Every year, so far without fail, I have had to respond to some acquaintance from my father's past who wishes him a happy birthday on social media, not knowing he passed away three years ago. Even though I have had to respond, I suppose I could just let the social media go and ignore it. However, I do not really want to see well wishes to my father in my Facebook newsfeed for the next ten or more years. I am certainly not where I was when people asked about him in the first few months after his death. That was a particularly dark place. Even three years later, however, I still have a twinge of physical and emotional pain that is, at the very least, buried a little deeper when his name comes up. I continue to make some sort of progress.

*

*The most beautiful people we have known*
*are those who have known defeat, known suffering,*
*known struggle, known loss, and have found their way out of those depths.*
ELISABETH KÜBLER-ROSS

\*

CHAPTER SIX

# THE DATES

*No matter what anyone says about grief and about time healing*
*all wounds, the truth is, there are certain sorrows that never fade*
*away until the heart stops beating and the last breath is taken.*
UNKNOWN

Our expectations and memories of balloons and cakes and presents are as regular as the rising sun. When our parent passes, however, how do we celebrate the life that is no more? And how do we acknowledge the painful date that marks their death?

*

SOPHIE BLOWERS
Sophie was 50 when her mother Amy
died at age 79 of internal bleeding

It has only been nine months since I lost my mom, so I have not experienced the one year mark. I know with my father's passing, I would get very grumpy on the anniversary of his death, even if I did not realize what day it was. I would analyze why I was in such a foul mood and suddenly see the date. It is amazing that we may try to tuck these dates, anniversaries, and memories into the far corners of our mind, but the subconscious knows they have to come out.

\*

## CHRISTINE DUMINIAK
Christine was 57 when her mother Ann
died at age 86 from an abdominal aortic aneurysm

On the death anniversary, my sister and I will contact each other to acknowledge it. For my parents' birthdays, I have a Catholic mass said in their honor at our parish church.

\*

## WENDY EVANS
Wendy was 14 when her father Dwight
died at age 32 in a plane crash

For around twenty-five years, my brothers and I called each other on October 8 and February 3, which are the birth and death dates of our father. We have not kept up the practice recently. One of my brothers and I have both lost sons at a young age. Our focus is more on the events of our son's passing.

\*

## BONNIE FORSHEY
Bonnie was an infant when her father Andrew
died at age 41 from a cerebral hemorrhage
Bonnie was 60 when her mother Doris
died at age 81 from colon cancer

I take flowers to the cemetery and also say a prayer on that day. I miss them but can't bring them back.

\*

## SKIP FRANKLIN
Skip was 41 when his mother Dianne
died at age 63 from a series of physical issues

I don't even remember the exact date of my mother's passing, sometime near the end of September. One of my sisters thinks it was October 3, the birthday of my oldest son. I know exactly where I was when it happened and what I went through, and I think that is what I hold on to. In terms of celebration, that occurs on my mom's birthday, July 27. I like to grab a coffee in her honor. I miss being able to take my mom out for coffee at a pastry shop and enjoy a nice long talk. We have a lot to catch up on. Sometimes I do that on Mother's Day as well.

\*

DONNA GORE
Donna was 26 when her father Donald
died by homicide in 1980

I may go to the cemetery and bring a plant. However, in more recent years, as a prolific writer, it is my pleasure and passion to write about crime as a tribute to him with a creative bent with each and every anniversary and milestone. We have no particular family ritual. However, this may be a function of our differences in generation, personalities and coping styles. Given that my mother is in her eighties and a private person by nature, it is still upsetting for her to this day. Fond memories come easily in conversation, but the tragic nature of the circumstances of the murder is generally not discussed often in my family, as is her unspoken preference.

\*

KIMBERLY HAWKS
Kimberly was 9 when her father Charles
died at age 32 in a car accident

My daddy died in late April, and on the anniversary of his passing I say a prayer for him. We have a little chat together. I tell him I forgive him and I love him and I miss him.

\*

VICKI HECKROTH
Vicki was 5 when her mother Bonnie
died at age 27 in an auto accident

November will always be hard for me. Not only was it the month my mother died, it is also the month when my seventeen-year-old son completed suicide. I cry in private a lot during the holidays, both for my son and the closeness I wish I had with my mother. When I was younger, I would reach my arms for the heavens as I cried, wanting just one more hug.

I do not have a close relationship with my parents any longer. My stepmom is a Jehovah's Witness and I am dis-fellowshipped due to an unscriptural divorce and then living with my current husband before we married. So my stepmom is not supposed to talk to me or have any association. I could go back to the church, as I am married now, however they could not speak to me until I was reinstated. I am happy now just being a Christian. I cannot believe in any religion that tears families apart like that.

My father and I have not had a close relationship since I was a troubled teenager. Like he told me a few years back, I destroyed that relationship when I got messed up in drugs and attempted suicide. That was over forty years ago and he still has not gotten over it. I also went against his wishes when I married my high school sweetheart. He told me if I did it, it would be over his dead body. Never say that to a rebellious teenager. I married the day before I graduated high school. My parents did not come to my wedding or my graduation.

\*

TERESA HERRING
Teresa was 47 when her father Burton
died at age 65 from brain cancer

Honestly I have no idea when my father's birthday is. I have never celebrated it with him. I do remember visiting his home once and on the wall was a framed picture where everyone signed it for his birthday. I remember thinking at the time, "Why wasn't I invited?" As usual, I wasn't asked to sign it. I sent him a birthday card a few times, but don't recall ever calling him or talking to him on his birthday. I do remember once calling his home and my stepsister answered. I asked to speak to Dad and she said, "You have the wrong number." Wow, that hurt. I had to tell her who I was before she realized her mistake.

\*

BROOKE NINNI MATTHEWS
Brooke was 38 when her mother JoAnne
died at age 57 from cardiac arrhythmia

I acknowledge my mom's birthday and angelversary, as I like to call it, with a cake or making one of her favorite meals, or going to one of her favorite restaurants. Her birthday and death day are both in August, so my family might go to the beach on her birthday or angelversary, because she loved the beach. It's just those little things to let her know that we honor and celebrate her. Depending on the day, that rollercoaster of grief influences my emotions on those important days.

\*

RUTH PAPALAS
Ruth was 41 when her father David
died at age 62 of a heart attack

My sisters and I usually post a tribute and sometimes some photos on Facebook.

*

MARY LEE ROBINSON
Mary Lee was 56 when her father Pat
died at age 82 of a massive cerebral hemorrhage

I am reminded of Dad's death every tax day, April 15. My husband was an accountant and tax season was extremely busy for him, and by extension, for us. Dad thoughtfully passed away the day after busy season was over. I don't do anything special, but I often chuckle at his thoughtfulness. It was just like him. As for Dad's birthday, that is a little harder. My husband's birthday was the day after Dad's. Those two days can be tough. I generally plan a quiet couple of days at home. I doubt those two days will ever be easy, and I don't expect to do anything differently.

*

PATTI SULLIVAN
Patti was 14 when her father Alfred
died at age 61 from a heart attack

I just kind of remember my dad's birthday by telling my husband or child. The death of my dad shows up every year, it just kind of comes to me. My family said he died the last day of summer, that sticks in my head. Sometimes I cry, forty-three years later.

*

JUDY TAYLOR
Judy was 55 when her mum Shirley
died at age 78 from a stroke

In everyday life I have many rituals to help me stay connected with my mum. As birthdays, Christmas and anniversaries come around, I open my heart to different ways to make her part of the celebration. Some of my family join me in keeping the traditions alive, others do their own thing. There are always mixed emotions at these times and I do my best to be in the moment and allow my feelings to flow.

\*

ALEXIS VON UTTER
Alexis was 12 when her father Marc
died at age 57 from lung cancer complications

We usually buy cupcakes or even just ignore it, we try to stay to ourselves in our household and if we celebrate, it gets to be too much.

\*

HEATHER WALLACE-REY
Heather was 40 when her father John
died suddenly at age 71 of a massive heart attack

For the first anniversary of my father's death, his first birthday without him, and the first holidays without him, I felt well prepared. People who had previously been there had prepared me. They prepared me by telling me it would be easier if I mentally and emotionally completely thought through these days before they arrived.

For the first anniversary of my dad's death and his birthday, this worked exceptionally well. While I was unable to plan how I would feel or my emotional state, I preplanned those particular days that first year. I planned to do things that my dad would have loved: planted flowers, went to lunch, read a book, hung out with my kids. Those particular days were preplanned enough that they became days that I was able to celebrate his life instead of mourning his death.

My second year anniversaries (and birthdays and holidays) were actually much more difficult because I had not considered the fact that I was not yet "over" grief (because you get over it like a cold or the flu, right?), and the anniversary of his death snuck up on me, and I had no plans. I might as well have stayed in bed all day long with the covers over my head. I was worthless to everyone all day.

Now I preplan every anniversary of his death and his birthday. It helps. It doesn't always make me completely emotion-free, but it gives me a clear purpose and defined things to do to celebrate his life on those days. It keeps me moving, which can also be considered some sort of progress. My dad would be particularly unhappy if he thought I was wallowing in some sort of self-pity instead of doing something productive on those days.

The summer after my dad's passing, I embarked on the biggest project to keep me busy that I have ever done: I researched and planted a butterfly garden in my yard, in memory of my dad. The more grief that was present that summer, the more plants I bought and got from friends. The more misery I felt, the more I put into the garden. Our neighbors and friends continually stop by to tell us how gorgeous this garden is but - if you look closely - there are about a million plants in that garden. If you look closely enough, it's not really one of the most beautiful gardens you've ever seen; it looks much more like what happens when someone with a semi-green thumb has a nervous breakdown. This garden is both a blessing and a curse. It is a great project to get to work on during those days that are emotionally difficult but it is also an ongoing project that requires time and attention all year long. This garden is the thing that "saved me from myself" (and from grieving) that first summer, but is now often the bane of my existence with how much continual maintenance it requires.

*

CHAPTER SEVEN

# THE HOLIDAYS

*The only predictable thing about grief*
*is that it's unpredictable.*
LYNDA CHELDELIN FELL

The holiday season comes around like clockwork, and for those in mourning, this time of year brings a kaleidoscope of emotions. If the grief is still fresh, the holidays can be downright raw. How do we navigate the invitations, decorations, and festivities that conjure up memories of yesteryear?

\*

SOPHIE BLOWERS
Sophie was 50 when her mother Amy
died at age 79 of internal bleeding

Christmas will be brutal this year. This will be the first Christmas without mom. She would always come and stay with my family for the month of December, so I am dreading this year without her. I think I may wear her slippers on Christmas morning, the slippers and bathrobe were so much a part of her. I don't know if it will be a sweet or bitter way to memorialize her. I may have to wait until Christmas morning to decide.

*

CHRISTINE DUMINIAK
Christine was 57 when her mother Ann
died at age 86 from an abdominal aortic aneurysm

The first year that my father died, it was extremely painful and sorrowful when the holidays came around. The very first holiday was Easter. I was dreading seeing my dad's empty chair at my mother's house. However, my brother-in-law took it upon himself to sit in my dad's usual chair. At first I was shocked. Then my next emotion was relief and gratitude. Why? Because I did not have to look at my dad's chair being empty. We had all the holidays at my parents' house, so when my mother passed four years after my dad, we were no longer able to celebrate the holidays at my parents. My two sisters and I divided up the holidays and we each celebrate one in our home. It was strange at first, but we have all settled into the new normal, and after the first year of change, have gotten used to spending the holidays at one another's home. We are happy that we can still all be together and we do feel our parents' presence with us. The holiday rituals are pretty much the same. We have tried to keep the tradition as close as possible to what we always did. That familiarity seems to help too.

*

WENDY EVANS
Wendy was 14 when her father Dwight
died at age 32 in a plane crash

In the 1970s, we celebrated holidays at my mother's home. We did have conversations about Dad but since my mother was remarried we did not talk about it as much for fear of hurting our mom's husband. After we started our own families, two of us moved away from Mom. Our holidays are primarily with our individual families now. If we can be together we definitely do it. The three of us remain very close to our mother. She has actually lived with my youngest brother for over twenty years.

\*

BONNIE FORSHEY
Bonnie was an infant when her father Andrew
died at age 41 from a cerebral hemorrhage
Bonnie was 60 when her mother Doris
died at age 81 from colon cancer

Christmas is harder for me because my mother loved it. I also have a difficult time on Mother's Day. They are all hard.

\*

SKIP FRANKLIN
Skip was 41 when his mother Dianne
died at age 63 from a series of physical issues

Of the holidays, I would say Thanksgiving comes to mind the most. My mom prepared some great dishes for the occasion. All of my siblings have done a great job carrying on the tradition. And so it really doesn't matter where we end up having Thanksgiving, there is definitely a sense of Mom's influence there. Christmas is very similar. It resembles very much what we grew up with. It is more comforting than painful. In fact, I would say it's a loving tribute to Mom, filled with joy and peace.

\*

DONNA GORE
Donna was 26 when her father Donald
died by homicide in 1980

Our specific traditions in terms of family gatherings have continued pretty much as they had prior to the homicide, with the inclusion of one grandchild and daughter-in law that my father never had the opportunity to meet. As the holiday season approaches, those of us who are the veteran survivors of crime are cognizant of the flood of emotions evoked on Thanksgiving, Hanukah, Christmas and the New Year's holidays… as well as anniversary dates.

Those who have recently been accosted by violent crime, for the first time experience a vacuous holiday season without their loved one. Holidays that once held meaning, are no more. Survivors of crime say to them, "What's the point anymore?"

At some point it hits us that we have to face the holidays. They will come no matter what has occurred before. What to do about that empty seat at the dinner table? What to do about the gifts you can't bring yourself to buy and the little rituals your beloved "always took care of." Our surviving relatives may be able to function, but we can't. Our friends try to pick up the slack by offering to do anything needed.

\*

KIMBERLY HAWKS
Kimberly was 9 when her father Charles
died at age 32 in a car accident

I still struggle a bit during the holiday season. Because my daddy was born on Christmas Day, it makes it extra tough. This is something I have no control over, so I just have to deal with it. But I love singing at Christmas time in memory of my dad and in honor of God who helped me get through all of this.

\*

VICKI HECKROTH
Vicki was 5 when her mother Bonnie
died at age 27 in an auto accident

I just make sure the holidays are enjoyable for everyone, and that I am the mother and grandmother that I know my own mother would have been. I do my best to make her proud of me and the person I have become. If I know someone is going to be alone for the holidays, I invite them to my home to spend it with us. I also adopt three to four families per year to make sure their holidays are special. I just wish I had the means to be able to do more.

92

*

TERESA HERRING
Teresa was 47 when her father Burton
died at age 65 from brain cancer

When I was a young adult, dad used to send me Christmas cards with cash in them. That happened for a few years. I always got my feelings hurt that even though we lived in the same city I was never invited for Christmas, Thanksgiving or any holiday ever. Not dinner, not anything. In my mind I know it was because I would see what gifts they exchanged or they did not want to spend the money on me. I think Christmas will always be the most painful memories of all the holidays.

*

BROOKE NINNI MATTHEWS
Brooke was 38 when her mother JoAnne
died at age 57 from cardiac arrhythmia

I think the holidays are hard, but not any harder than any other day. Grief comes in waves and depending on the wave that comes through that day, my emotions mirror that day's wave. Our family used to get together for the big holidays like Thanksgiving, Easter, Christmas Eve and Christmas. But since the death of my mother, we kind of do our own thing with our husbands, kids and friends for holidays. My mother was and always will be the rock and bond that holds our family together.

*

RUTH PAPALAS
Ruth was 41 when her father David
died at age 62 of a heart attack

Holidays will never be the same. The first Easter after Dad died, I automatically placed my "standing order" for a Daffin's chocolate nut egg and a box of chocolate-covered caramels for my dad. And then I cried. Strangely for me, Father's Day is when I miss

Dad most. When I see the Father's Day cards and realize I will never purchase one again, it brings tears to my eyes. Sometimes I still read the cards and look for the one I would have purchased if Dad were still here. When I go to church and they are honoring all the dads, I miss mine the most. Dad loved Halloween and loved to buy and hand out giant licorice sticks because he loved to watch the kids' faces light up. Mom kept that up for a while. Now the treats have shrunk to small pieces of candy.

Thanksgiving is still my favorite holiday. My sisters and I all go to Mom's for a great time and a delicious meal. It has a whole different feel, though. At Christmas our family always got together and my brothers would travel home for one, either Thanksgiving or Christmas. Now the boys don't come home, Mom goes to them. It is not the same. It never will be.

*

MARY POTTER KENYON
Mary was 26 when her father Byron died at age 61 following a fall
Mary was 51 when her mother Irma died at age 82 from lung cancer

The first Thanksgiving after my mother's death was spent with my extended family at my house. We needed to be together. That Christmas was worse for me, since I spent it in the hospital where my five-year-old grandson was recovering from surgery to remove cancer. I was just numb with grief and shock. Christmas was always spent at my mother's and that option was suddenly pulled away from us. Now, I spend both Thanksgiving and Christmas with my own eight children, but I like to visit or see my siblings during the holiday season too.

\*

MARY LEE ROBINSON
Mary Lee was 56 when her father Pat
died at age 82 of a massive cerebral hemorrhage

The holidays can bring a profound sense of being alone. That is alleviated by the kindness of friends who realized my plight after a time, and now include me at their table. My husband and I always toasted our departed parents on special holidays. That usually spurred some sharing of special memories as well.

\*

PATTI SULLIVAN
Patti was 14 when her father Alfred
died at age 61 from a heart attack

Our core family died when my dad died. I see it happening with my father-in-law's recent death. Dads are the glue of the family. I tried to continue family traditions for years. When our daughter became a drug addict and caused our family so much trauma, I didn't care about that stuff. The recession killed a lot of our dreams as well.

\*

JUDY TAYLOR
Judy was 55 when her mum Shirley
died at age 78 from a stroke

In Australia there seems to be holidays, anniversaries and birthdays throughout the year and I am aware of Mum's presence as each one approaches. Sometimes my emotions and feelings take me completely by surprise so I allow myself to acknowledge each event as it approaches and be aware that feelings will surface. I give myself extra nurturing time to help me through the painful moments.

\*

### ALEXIS VON UTTER
Alexis was 12 when her father Marc
died at age 57 from lung cancer complications

All holidays are the hardest, but mostly Thanksgiving and Christmas. My dad was a huge cook and it is difficult not having him cooking that huge meal anymore. Christmas is hard as well due to the fact that it was such a huge family gathering for us.

\*

### HEATHER WALLACE-REY
Heather was 40 when her father John
died suddenly at age 71 of a massive heart attack

While I suppose that much of celebrating holiday traditions hinges on the stage in life that your family is in, I feel lucky that my dad's death came at a time when my children were all teenagers and young adults and we were moving out of state, both of which naturally disrupted the flow of the way we do holidays. If all of our family traditions had changed solely based on the death of my father, I think I would still be much more emotional, especially at Christmas. Christmas Eve is often difficult. At our church's Christmas Eve worship services, there are families who have three or four generations attending worship together. It is difficult to see a senior citizen with his arm wrapped around his daughter and his granddaughter without thinking, "I will never have that. My children will never have that." In those moments, I try to remember how blessed I was to have my dad until he was 71.

\*

CHAPTER EIGHT

# THE BELONGINGS

*Of all possessions, a friend is the most precious.*
HERODOTUS

Our parent's belongings are a direct connection to what once was. Many of us are, at some point, tasked with accepting that the tangible souvenirs from our childhood are material items that, cherished or not, must be dealt with. When does the time come to address the task of sorting our parent's memory-laden belongings, and how does one begin?

*

SOPHIE BLOWERS
Sophie was 50 when her mother Amy
died at age 79 of internal bleeding

My mother's belongings are still packed in boxes consuming my basement. We initially put them in storage partially for convenience, partially for avoidance. Finally I had to make the long twelve-hour drive to go get the last of the items from my mom's household. It was especially hard because as I left, I knew there would never be a reason for me to return to that part of Florida. It felt like a double kick to the gut. I kept saying, "There are too many last times."

The funny thing my sister and I noticed was the type of things we kept. I kept my mother's hospital badge from when she was a volunteer, her bedspread and her prayer book. Things my mother touched meant the most. She had lovely jewelry, but rarely wore it... I did not want any of it. I wanted her watch that she never took off. I am both dreading and looking forward to going through the boxes. It will be very hard, but I am hoping that with a glass of wine in hand, I can laugh with mom and say, "Oh Mom, what was I thinking when I kept this?" I know my mom, the eternal neat freak, will be prodding me to get rid of much of it. I may; I may not. For now I will have her badge on my nightstand, her watch on my wrist, her comforter to surround me at night and her voice saying, "What were you thinking?"

*

CHRISTINE DUMINIAK
Christine was 57 when her mother Ann
died at age 86 from an abdominal aortic aneurysm

When my dad passed, my mother asked us to clean out his bedroom for her. So my sisters and our husbands did that. My mother gave just about everything to charity. But then later regretted that there seemed to be physically nothing left of our dad in the house. After my mother passed, my sisters and I got together to go through her belongings. Anything that anyone liked when it came to my mother's clothes and jewelry, we asked each other for permission, if it was okay for us to take that particular item. We also gave some of my mother's things to her personal friends. When it came to large pieces of furniture, some of the items we kept for ourselves. Some of the large items we gave to others who we knew could use them. The rest we gave to charity.

*

WENDY EVANS
Wendy was 14 when her father Dwight
died at age 32 in a plane crash

I do not recall how my father's belongings were handled. I do know that I still have his bowling ball, case and bowling shoes. I also have his briefcase. I am not sure where the other belongings went, and I have never asked my brothers if they have something of Dad's.

*

BONNIE FORSHEY
Bonnie was an infant when her father Andrew
died at age 41 from a cerebral hemorrhage
Bonnie was 60 when her mother Doris
died at age 81 from colon cancer

When my mother became ill, I spent so much time taking care of her. My two half-sisters conspired against me, and got power of attorney. I had no idea that this was even going on. I was in the hospital for tests when they took my mother to their home, and cleaned out her home, placing everything in storage. My mother was kept in a small bedroom on the second floor, unable to go down the stairs. I didn't get to see her again. My half-sisters did this just to make sure that I didn't get anything. I didn't even get my mother's photos of my children. I will never be able to forgive them for this. They kept me from my mother, when she was on her deathbed.

*

SKIP FRANKLIN
Skip was 41 when his mother Dianne
died at age 63 from a series of physical issues

Well, I had little use for Mom's clothing and accessories, so I left that up to my sisters. The one thing that was important was the Steinway grand piano that my mom and I both played. It was to go to me, and it did. I was living out of town and already had a piano, so we left it at Dad's. It was a 1904 Steinway and needed a lot of work. A Hollywood couple now owns the huge Tudor house that my grandfather built, and where my mom lived as a young child. They have basically adopted our family and bought from us many of the original furniture pieces that my mom had been saving. The Steinway is now on exhibit there as well. I was over there playing it not too long ago. It was totally refurbished and never sounded better.

*

DONNA GORE
Donna was 26 when her father Donald
died by homicide in 1980

I have specific memories regarding certain belongings. One of my most vivid memories is from shortly after the homicide. I'm not sure if it was at the medical examiner's office, or the Hartford police station. However, the circumstances surrounding the murder all seemed surreal to me, as if it was a movie on television, not really true at all. The pivotal moment when I realized it was indeed true was when a police station staff member walked out of the room carrying a plastic bag with my dad's coat, the one he wore the night of the murder. I suddenly realized it was true. He was gone!

Prior to his death, one of the vehicles my father owned was a green van for work purposes. As he was killed in his van, as it appeared in a newspaper article, it was part of the evidence for the trial. For many weeks after, when driving in traffic, if I saw a similar van or green colored vehicle, I experienced great anxiety, as if I was having a flashback.

My father's "claim to fame" was that he was a skilled New England motorcycles champion for many years, and attending weekly Sunday motorcycle races was part of the fabric of our lives. He accumulated a wealth of gleaming gold, marble, and mahogany trophies of every shape and size. I chose one as a memento.

A few years ago, my mother gave me a Christmas present consisting of a framed black and white photo of my smiling dad and me during his early days of racing. I was seated proudly on his motorcycle with my full-length gleaming metal leg braces which I wore as a child because of my spastic cerebral palsy.

*

KIMBERLY HAWKS
Kimberly was 9 when her father Charles
died at age 32 in a car accident

I was so young I really wasn't part of the process of going through my daddy's belongings. But I did end up with some little items that are very special to me. I use them for inspiration. And they definitely remind me of him and our family when I was young.

*

VICKI HECKROTH
Vicki was 5 when her mother Bonnie
died at age 27 in an auto accident

My grandmother kept my mother's clothes for my sister and I so we could see how tiny she was. They got to the point where they fell apart from being so old, however it was nice to be able to see them. I thought I was small at that time, being five feet tall and 105 pounds, but her clothes were too small even for me. I gave my mother's Catholic rosary to my oldest daughter Heidi, and my dad's rosary to my youngest daughter Melissa. My sister has our mother's wedding ring which she used as her own. My dad's wedding ring was buried with my son. I am not sure what happened to my mother's other things.

*

TERESA HERRING
Teresa was 47 when her father Burton
died at age 65 from brain cancer

I have never owned anything that belonged to my father. I did find out by accident that my sister was given something of importance that belonged to my father, which hurt my feelings a little. After he passed, my stepmother sent me some type of flower vase that was supposed to have been given to my mother at the hospital when I was born. I really doubt that it was given to my mother and that she had kept it all these years, especially with the bad feelings between her and my mother. It is still at my sister's house. I didn't want it and haven't asked for her to send it to me either. I have no emotions connected to it, so it will stay at my sister's house. I have had thoughts about getting it just to destroy it as some type of healing ritual, as crazy as that may sound.

*

BROOKE NINNI MATTHEWS
Brooke was 38 when her mother JoAnne
died at age 57 from cardiac arrhythmia

My siblings and I cleaned out my mom's house together, and we divided her belongs up between my mom's children, my mom's brother and sisters, and my mom's grandchildren.

*

RUTH PAPALAS
Ruth was 41 when her father David
died at age 62 of a heart attack

Mom had always joked with Dad and told him that if he died before her, that the first thing to go would be his boat and then the camper. When Dad unexpectedly died, Mom followed through. The boat went first followed almost immediately by the camper. I think all five of us kids were okay with that, as both were totally

Dad's. None of us five kids knew how to, nor wanted to, take care of either the boat or camper. We enjoyed the occasional use, but Dad always did all of the work. He used both often.

We had already gone through Dad's belongings and taken what we wanted and stuff Mom said was okay to take. Several months later, we had our annual garage sale. We had a lot of Dad's tools, fishing items and other miscellaneous items in the sale. Mom also put Dad's clothes in the sale. I was okay with all of that. When a man came and tried on one of my dad's favorite suit jackets on, I burst into tears. I couldn't take it. Mom then donated the rest of his clothing to a charity. We each had taken items we wanted of Dad's. I kept my favorite fishing lure. Odd, but I could tell you more stories about fishing in Canada with my Grandpa and Dad while thinking about that fishing lure. Before Dad died, I had bought him one of those books that they inserted names into to tell a story. It was called *My Fishing Adventure*, and was a story about catching Wally Walleye. The story featured my dad fishing with his brother Lawrence, Pastor Blauser, and Jeff. My dad read the book out loud and was crying he was laughing so hard. I kept that book! Once my nephew got older, Mom gave him the signed basketball. We didn't keep much stuff but we have lots of pictures and even more memories.

*

MARY POTTER KENYON
Mary was 26 when her father Byron died at age 61 following a fall
Mary was 51 when her mother Irma died at age 82 from lung cancer

I wish we had taken more time going through my mother's things after her death in 2010. With nine siblings and so much sorting to do, it seems like we concentrated on dividing up her art pieces and bigger pieces of furniture and weren't sure what to do with all the little things. I ended up with a lot of her writing; unpublished manuscripts, notebooks and small journals. I treasure these things, but I am sure some things got thrown away as we went through them quickly. It is the little notes and her handwriting that is precious. Dad died so many years before her, so mom was the one who had gone through his things. I was pregnant when he died, and my mom gave me one of Dad's plaid flannel shirts to wear during that pregnancy, and it was one of my favorite things to wear. I don't know what I did with it after the baby was born.

\*

MARY LEE ROBINSON
Mary Lee was 56 when her father Pat
died at age 82 of a massive cerebral hemorrhage

Since I lived in a different state than my parents, my mother took care of disposing of the bulk of Dad's things. I know she had help from friends. She did put aside some things for me to go through, and I kept a few. I have his Army insignia and his Bronze Star, a lot of photos, and some jewelry that belonged to his mother. I refer to her as his mother because she died before I was born. I never met her.

I cherish the family things that have been passed down to me from both sides of my family. I do remember going to visit Mom about six months later, and she told me that it bothered her to see Daddy's picture on her nightstand all through the day. They were married fifty-seven years. She asked if I would mind if she put it away. I told her to do whatever she needed to do to heal, of course. Not much longer after that, she decided to move out of the apartment she and Dad shared to a smaller unit one floor down and further down the hall. The decision was not solely financial. The big dilemma I have now is what plans to make for those things after I die. As an only child with little family, they don't mean much to anyone but me. Yet it is discomforting to think of them being cast away as insignificant.

\*

PATTI SULLIVAN
Patti was 14 when her father Alfred
died at age 61 from a heart attack

When my dad died my older sister gave me his ring. One day she said she wanted it back. Dumb little sister that I am, I gave it to her. What do I have of his? Some cards and a money clip. My older sisters took and took and took. That is their nature. They have his stuff, I had his time.

\*

JUDY TAYLOR
Judy was 55 when her mum Shirley
died at age 78 from a stroke

My dad and some of my sisters coordinated my mum's belongings. Everyone was given some time and space to choose some of her things. Family issues made it difficult for everyone to be together in this process. I feel I embraced every emotion and feeling I know through this time. I can feel them now as I write.

\*

HEATHER WALLACE-REY
Heather was 40 when her father John
died suddenly at age 71 of a massive heart attack

My dad had moved to a small apartment about a year before his death. Lucky for us, he did not own much in the way of furniture or trinkets. I have been at estate sales where I have often wondered how people manage to collect so many things and why they don't seem to get rid of the things they no longer want or need, long before death. In my dad's case, most of the things he collected were books, because he loved reading and inspired all six of his children to be pretty avid readers.

Dad was also into karate and Japanese weaponry. He had a pretty impressive collection of what my brothers and sisters and I fondly referred to as "ninja swords." The entire collection of "ninja swords" went to one of my younger brothers who was really interested in them. Before his passing, my dad never let my brothers (or my sisters or me) touch the weapons. By then, even my youngest brother was in his twenties. In hindsight, as much as it may have looked like an episode of a sitcom-gone-wrong, allowing the "trial run" of these weapons to happen in the living room of my dad's apartment, after his death was probably not a good choice. Having a small apartment full of people packing and moving boxes while one or two members of the team have officially become "the last Samurai" and can wait no longer to run through the apartment trying out weaponry was both hilarious and dangerous. At least three of my dad's children really did not want ninja swords in their house for fear of what our own children might do with them. We took turns picking which of Dad's books we each wanted to keep, and we gave some of his books to other people in his life that we knew Dad would have wanted them to have.

I have heard horror stories of division of things being an issue that has split families during times of grief, but material possessions have never been the focus of our lives. The most touching part of going through my dad's belongings was this: my dad had a giant file cabinet where he kept all sorts of things we never knew he kept: cards we made him in elementary school, our report cards, newspaper clippings from our plays and sporting events, programs from our band and orchestra and choir concerts, nice notes that people sent him, letters we had sent him from camp, even letters that his own mother had sent him when he was in the military. We packed up many of these because all six of us (my brothers and sisters and I) were so touched by these things.

\*

# CHAPTER NINE

# THE DARKNESS

*Walking with a friend in the dark*
*is better than walking alone in the light.*
HELEN KELLER

Sometimes suicidal thoughts occur in the immediate aftermath of a profound loss, yet few readily admit it for fear of being judged or condemned. While there would be no rainbow without the rain, where do we find the energy to fight the storm?

\*

SOPHIE BLOWERS
Sophie was 50 when her mother Amy
died at age 79 of internal bleeding

I have often struggled with depression. I would cut when stress got out of hand, just to have control over the pain I felt. I never considered suicide due to Mom's passing, but I did sometimes wish God would take me. I just wanted the hurt to stop. I wanted, and still want, the images of those last hours to disappear. I am coming to terms with it now, the images come less often and I can shoo them away quicker. I am finding joy and allow myself to breathe. I have a long way to go, but I am moving. Sometimes I move forward, sometimes backward, but at least I am moving.

\*

CHRISTINE DUMINIAK
Christine was 57 when her mother Ann
died at age 86 from an abdominal aortic aneurysm

No thoughts of suicide.

\*

WENDY EVANS
Wendy was 14 when her father Dwight
died at age 32 in a plane crash

Not related to my father's death. Wanting to die and thinking of suicide are two different things to me. After my son's death I thought about dying.

\*

BONNIE FORSHEY
Bonnie was an infant when her father Andrew
died at age 41 from a cerebral hemorrhage
Bonnie was 60 when her mother Doris
died at age 81 from colon cancer

I have not thought about suicide, but have definitely been depressed. I never thought that I would not have been able to say goodbye. Your mother is the first person to love you. I think about her so much, the things we did together, places we went. She gave me away when I was young, but I have been able to forgive her for that. She probably saved my life. It wasn't her fault. She did what she had to do, at the time.

*

SKIP FRANKLIN
Skip was 41 when his mother Dianne
died at age 63 from a series of physical issues

As discussed earlier in the book, I did find myself in a cloud of darkness and heaviness and a total loss of ambition. It was hypnotic really. It did not happen immediately after mom's passing, it crept in several days later. I would like to discuss the process of how this darkness dissipated, but it was a very immediate and alarming process which I recounted earlier. It was life-changing. And no, there has never been a recurrence of that darkness since. That was the end of that.

*

DONNA GORE
Donna was 26 when her father Donald
died by homicide in 1980

I had no suicidal ideation or attempts regarding the homicide.

*

KIMBERLY HAWKS
Kimberly was 9 when her father Charles
died at age 32 in a car accident

We all have our emotional challenges, and I am no exception. I was only nine when my dad passed and I don't recall any struggles then. And the struggles that I had in my adult years, it's hard to know how much of that stems from my dad's death. For years I had a mental barrier of reaching thirty-two years of age, which was my dad's age when the accident occurred. I think as I approached that age there was a delayed impact that affected me and my view of mortality and my readiness to leave this place and to "go home."

\*

### VICKI HECKROTH
Vicki was 5 when her mother Bonnie
died at age 27 in an auto accident

Yes, I thought about suicide and have made several attempts. I always had that urge to just go be with my mother growing up. I missed that love and bond that all my friends had with their mothers.

\*

### TERESA HERRING
Teresa was 47 when her father Burton
died at age 65 from brain cancer

Yes, it is hard to say how much of an influence this relationship had to do with my attempted suicide but I do think that had I had a healthy father-daughter relationship it may have influenced my decision. I think my attempt comes from a combination of the childhood feeling of not being good enough to be loved by my parents, and the fact that as an adult I never really got over the thoughts that if my parents didn't love me then who would? I don't blame the fact that I tried to kill myself on my parents' lack of love solely, for me it was the perfect storm of my childhood and the current circumstances at the time that led to my attempt.

Would a healthy relationship with my father have changed the attempt? Would I have reached out to him for support? Perhaps, but I will never know for sure. More likely than not, my suicide attempt had more to do with a chemical imbalance than anything else but the factors of my childhood made it easier to just give up.

\*

BROOKE NINNI MATTHEWS
Brooke was 38 when her mother JoAnne
died at age 57 from cardiac arrhythmia

I haven't had any thoughts of suicide after my mom's passing. It wasn't until my brother was murdered six months later that I and my daughter both had thoughts of suicide.

\*

RUTH PAPALAS
Ruth was 41 when her father David
died at age 62 of a heart attack

No. Never.

\*

MARY LEE ROBINSON
Mary Lee was 56 when her father Pat
died at age 82 of a massive cerebral hemorrhage

Suicide never entered my mind in conjunction with losing my father.

\*

PATTI SULLIVAN
Patti was 14 when her father Alfred
died at age 61 from a heart attack

Nope! Food is my go-to drug of choice.

\*

JUDY TAYLOR
Judy was 55 when her mum Shirley
died at age 78 from a stroke

No.

*

HEATHER WALLACE-REY
Heather was 40 when her father John
died suddenly at age 71 of a massive heart attack

I have never been much of a suicidal person. If anything, I used to regularly be accused by my friends of being the Pollyanna of the group: I like to try to see the positive in everything. Maybe it is just fortunate for me that death and grief are two of the only things in all of my life that I couldn't put a positive spin on. Before I sought professional help, I did have a few days where I was physically unable to get out of bed, and I heard the whispers of my friends and family as they tried to decide how to tell me that they thought I was depressed. I already knew I was depressed, I just didn't know how to deal with it. I like things that can be fixed, things you can slap a bandage and some Neosporin on and just let them heal. I initially thought grief would be like that: you would spend a few weeks healing and then wake up one day and be better. The unfamiliarity of depression and the hard work it takes to overcome it was really difficult for me.

I never wished to end my own life, although I would be lying if I didn't admit to having some moments where I considered that if I didn't have to wake up the next morning then I wouldn't have to feel the immense pain in my heart anymore. My struggle has been less about whether or not I should continue to exist, but HOW I can continue to not only exist, but get back to enjoying and largely seeing the positive things in life.

*

CHAPTER TEN

# THE FRIENDS

*Remember, you don't need a certain number of friends,*
*just a number of friends you can be certain of.*
UNKNOWN

When we are mourning, some of our friendships undergo transitions. Some bonds remain steady, dependable and faithful. Some we sever by choice. And, perhaps unexpectedly, new friends enter our life, bringing renewed hope rich with possibilities. But what about your parent's friends? Do you keep in touch with them?

\*

SOPHIE BLOWERS
Sophie was 50 when her mother Amy
died at age 79 of internal bleeding

No, I am ashamed that I have not kept in touch with them. I know they are hurting and would love for me to be in their lives, but I am just not ready. I am being selfish, but I am allowing myself this self-preservation tactic. I will reach out soon. The holidays are coming and it will make sense for me to send cards and make calls. It will give me a gradual entry into some of their lives, and into memories of mom before she became ill.

\*

## CHRISTINE DUMINIAK
Christine was 57 when her mother Ann
died at age 86 from an abdominal aortic aneurysm

I have had some interaction with my mother's good friends. When I did, I felt a closeness to them because they loved my mother too. It was so nice to hear them talk about my mother.

\*

## WENDY EVANS
Wendy was 14 when her father Dwight
died at age 32 in a plane crash

I am sure I did have interaction with my father's friends after he passed. As in most cases, my father's friends who pledged to always be there for us kids eventually faded away. I have no contact with anyone who was friends with my father. I always like it when someone from my hometown mentions that they knew my dad. The stories are fun to hear and it feels good that someone remembers him.

\*

## BONNIE FORSHEY
Bonnie was an infant when her father Andrew
died at age 41 from a cerebral hemorrhage
Bonnie was 60 when her mother Doris
died at age 81 from colon cancer

I have not seen any of my mother's friends. I stay to myself, it is just too painful any other way. I try desperately to block everything out. I am on antidepressants to help me cope with the loss.

\*

SKIP FRANKLIN
Skip was 41 when his mother Dianne
died at age 63 from a series of physical issues

The last time I saw most of my mom's friends was at her memorial service. It was wonderful seeing them all and hearing all of the great stories. I think because it was held over a month after Mom's passing, a lot of the heaviness had cleared and it was a very elevating and joyous occasion. Over the last ten years, my sisters have probably kept in touch with some of Mom's friends. They probably face more issues than I do.

\*

DONNA GORE
Donna was 26 when her father Donald
died by homicide in 1980

After so many years, I don't recall specifically about my father's friends. However, within the past month, I received an inquiry on my website from the daughter of one of my father's friends who took over one of his former businesses. She was investigating unsolved homicides and came across my information. She spoke of how upset her father was at my father's death. She revealed her father had since passed away as well. This was very touching to me. I responded and passed on the information to my mother, so that my mother might follow up as well. I have had other people reach out occasionally from my father's racing days, or in other contexts. Each time it is a precious connection.

\*

### KIMBERLY HAWKS
Kimberly was 9 when her father Charles
died at age 32 in a car accident

A few months after my dad's death, my mom remarried and we moved from Michigan down to New Mexico, away from my dad's family and friends. It's been twenty years since I've been to Michigan, and twenty years since I've seen my dad's family. I'm currently involved in a project that has brought me back to Michigan after all this time. In some ways it's full circle for me. I have not had the opportunity to locate any of my dad's family yet, but I'm looking forward to it. It's also a little scary, since I haven't seen them for so long.

\*

### VICKI HECKROTH
Vicki was 5 when her mother Bonnie
died at age 27 in an auto accident

I had a lot of interaction with my mother's best friend, Jolene, while growing up. My mother was killed in her driveway. Jolene and her husband Gary remained friends with my dad and stepmom until finally one day they stopped coming around. I never knew why or what happened. I always enjoyed seeing them as I was close with their daughter Darci, and they had known my mother personally. I remained close with her mother, my grandmother, and aunts, uncles and cousins growing up although I wasn't allowed to see them very often. When my son died, my Aunt Joyce gave us her plot so I could bury my son next to my mother. My aunt died ten months later from brain cancer, and had to be buried down the row from the family. I will never forget her generosity as it meant so much to me to have my son with my mother like that.

*

### TERESA HERRING
Teresa was 47 when her father Burton
died at age 65 from brain cancer

I do not know any of my father's friends but can say that since his passing his family, my stepmother and children, were at my niece's wedding. When I saw them, I stupidly went and hugged my stepmother. I regretted it almost immediately as she was stone cold in response. She and my stepsiblings avoided me the rest of the night. I watched other family members having conversations with them and I felt betrayed by my family. I felt as if they were siding with them. I felt alone, like no one understood my side of the decision I made.

*

### BROOKE NINNI MATTHEWS
Brooke was 38 when her mother JoAnne
died at age 57 from cardiac arrhythmia

I occasionally have interaction with my mom's friends, and I am friends with a few of them on Facebook.

*

### RUTH PAPALAS
Ruth was 41 when her father David
died at age 62 of a heart attack

We relocated so I don't have much opportunity to interact with many of Dad's old friends. Mom and Dad's old friends, sadly, did not remain Mom's friends. Some of my dad's friends have passed also. My daughter was born prematurely. The pastor that came to the neonatal ward and prayed for her eventually relocated. Recently he moved back to my mom's area. My daughter just had a premature baby. Mom just took her and her baby to see that same pastor, Pastor Blauser, my dad's friend who was mentioned in that book. My daughter sent me the picture. The smile on Pastor

Blauser's face made me cry. My dad and this pastor were fishing buddies and did fish fries for the men at church, told jokes, and just had fun together. That smile brought it all back and it has been over fifteen years now.

*

MARY LEE ROBINSON
Mary Lee was 56 when her father Pat
died at age 82 of a massive cerebral hemorrhage

I run into friends of my dad's every time I go home to visit Mom. It has been awhile, eight years since he died, so it's not very emotional. Initially, it was sweet when they brought his name up. They always told me what a gentleman he was and how much they missed him too. My parents are of a generation that was much better equipped to handle death, I think. They expected it, were not shocked by it, and harbored no silly notions that we are all supposed to live forever. They talk about it much more easily than my age group, for sure. They look at it as normal, and it usually is.

*

PATTI SULLIVAN
Patti was 14 when her father Alfred
died at age 61 from a heart attack

No, I was so young when he passed.

*

JUDY TAYLOR
Judy was 55 when her mum Shirley
died at age 78 from a stroke

In the early days, there was much interaction with several friends which has since tapered off; we shared some close friends. I continue to laugh, cry and enjoy life with these people just as we did when Mum was here. She is part of our conversation. I love that.

*

## HEATHER WALLACE-REY
Heather was 40 when her father John
died suddenly at age 71 of a massive heart attack

My dad's longtime girlfriend and I have communicated from time to time since his death. As it is with my siblings, it is still difficult for me to talk to her because my loss is also HER loss. She has three adult children that are about the same age as my siblings and I, and I used to get to see pictures of my dad on social media at her family gatherings, with her grandchildren, as well as at our family gatherings. I can still see her social media and I often see pictures of her family gatherings, particularly of her grandchildren, and I always feel this twinge (I try not to admit that every single thing I'm feeling is grief) because my dad used to talk about her grandchildren, especially one of the little boys, and how much fun they would have together. It is a little like watching a movie without your favorite character in it: there is an empty space in the pictures where my dad used to be. For the most part, I don't want to call her because I don't want to be HER reminder of my dad. My goal is not only to be able to fight my own grief, but also not to make anyone else's worse.

*

*How to survive grief:*
*One breath at a time.*
LYNDA CHELDELIN FELL

\*

CHAPTER ELEVEN

# THE RELATIONSHIPS

*I have found the paradox that if you love until it hurts,*
*there can be no more hurt, only more love.*
MOTHER TERESA

For many of us, familial relationships are the cornerstones that help us stay sane; they keep us laughing, learning, and loving. We speak one another's language and finish one another's sentences. Sometimes, however, loss touches us in different ways. What family relations, if any, were impacted by the loss of your parent?

\*

SOPHIE BLOWERS
Sophie was 50 when her mother Amy
died at age 79 of internal bleeding

The relationship with one of my siblings has been completely severed. I am still at a loss to even attempt to describe what happened. It is amazing how loss can bring out the best and the worst in people. I will not attempt to put motives to their actions, but I can only assume that guilt and anger can consume people and they have to find someone to blame so they do not implode. I am sad for my sibling. I really am. I am also at a point of self-survival.

The loss of Mom... the exhaustion of being a caregiver... I just can't coddle them right now. I feel sorry that there is such a negative legacy left from Mom's passing, but there is a point when we have to heal. Sometimes healing requires us to stop making everything okay for others and allow them to deal with grief in their own way, no matter how destructive or unhealthy it is. I must find my path, my healing journey and walk it. I would love others to join me, but I cannot and will not have the memory of someone I loved so much be entwined with negative and malicious emotions. Sometimes the best we can do is wear the oxygen mask ourselves and be prepared to share it when we are stronger. The one good thing that their attacks have done is helped me with some of my guilt from the "I should have" syndrome. Due to having to defend my actions, I realized that I gave my all to Mom. I would love to have a few do-overs, but 99.9 percent of my time as her caregiver, I have no regrets. I will not allow someone, even though they are grieving, to question my motives. Caring for Mom, holding her during those last hours, was the hardest thing I have ever done. Walking away and allowing someone else to tend to her would have been much easier, but then I would have nothing but regrets. I will take nightmares over regrets any day of the week.

*

CHRISTINE DUMINIAK<br>Christine was 57 when her mother Ann<br>died at age 86 from an abdominal aortic aneurysm

The loss of my father brought my mother and me even closer, but one of my sisters acted a little distant from us. My mother and I were receiving some afterlife signs from my dad. We found these signs to be extremely comforting. However, at that time my sister did not believe in afterlife signs, so she would walk out of the room when my mother and I were discussing our spiritual experiences. This bothered my mother greatly and was a little hurtful to me also. However, over time, my sister started to notice some very strong afterlife signs and this brought her closer to us again.

*

WENDY EVANS
Wendy was 14 when her father Dwight
died at age 32 in a plane crash

I had a permanent disconnect from the woman who was married to my dad for twenty-eight days, took all the money from the trust fund, and did not pay the funeral bill.

*

BONNIE FORSHEY
Bonnie was an infant when her father Andrew
died at age 41 from a cerebral hemorrhage
Bonnie was 60 when her mother Doris
died at age 81 from colon cancer

The loss of my mother has caused a permanent disconnect with my half-sisters. I tried to help my mother during her battle with cancer. I bought her medications, groceries, and took her to her appointments. I didn't grow up with my mother, so my half-sisters felt threatened. The youngest one talked my mother into making her the power of attorney. After my mother signed it, she took my mother out of her own home, and moved her into an upstairs bedroom of my half-sister's house. She then packed up all of my mother's belongings and put them in a storage unit. This was all done, to make sure that I didn't get anything, not even a photograph.

*

SKIP FRANKLIN
Skip was 41 when his mother Dianne
died at age 63 from a series of physical issues

There have been two greatly impacted relationships; one positive and one challenging. The positive one involved my two sisters. They are very different and were never close growing up. After my mom passed, they finally bonded after all these years. It was amazing to see them calling each other several times a week. I have to say, I envision my mom smiling at this constantly. While I can't see her saying the words, "This is wonderful! It was almost worth dying for!"...I can see her being very pleased. Everything comes full circle. The challenging one involved my dad. He was always my hero and I was just disappointed on how he handled that last six months of Mom's life. I really struggled with it. He is a fine man and a great role model, but he fell from his pedestal on this one. We were always close, so it did not cause a division, but it did take me a few years to resolve it. That part was challenging for me.

*

DONNA GORE<br>
Donna was 26 when her father Donald<br>
died by homicide in 1980

This is a difficult question to answer as I have had what most people would classify as numerous losses and tragedies in my life prior to the homicide, given a history of what now is fifty-eight surgeries. I am most proud of the fact that despite all of the unique childhood events I experienced, and although there was much personal sacrifice, missed opportunities, rejection and pain, my parents did everything possible to provide as normal a childhood as possible for all of us with things like swimming, music lessons, summer vacations at the beach, trips to New York City and other major attractions, love, family dinners etc. When you have a permanent physical, obvious disability, you pay the price socially. You are more vulnerable, subject to self-isolation, depression, rejection by others and more. You feel you have to work one thousand percent harder just to measure up to the rest of the pack. You are vulnerable, but you compensate with an intense drive to succeed. This has carried over to my adult life. I am very strong, but vulnerable too. I take some things too personally. I can face almost any situation, but intensely fear rejection from those I care for the most. Selected personal relationships have been hurtful, such that I vowed always to be single and never take the chance again.

From my point of view, my parents came together as a married couple but also had independent interests. I think this pattern also follows their three children. According to the classic definition, we are not close-knit as siblings or a family in comparison to most families. We lead very different and separate lives with separate interests. We get along and come together, mostly on major holidays. However, normal everyday communication is usually very limited between the three siblings except with my mother serving as the conduit, and sometimes message passer. This has always seemed very unique to me. I hope that my siblings didn't feel like second-class citizens, taking a backseat to all of my medical needs, but perhaps they did and it has carried over to our relationships as adults. I certainly had no control over such events. My parents did the very best they could to equalize things.

When the homicide occurred, I was the advocate, the spokesperson, the person who wanted all of the answers, the vocal one. I alone attended the three-week trial with my mother while my siblings chose to only attend the sentencing. We coped separately, differently. We had different points of view. As I became more active in the field of crime victim advocacy in Connecticut, and have achieved certain notoriety across the country in some circles, most of my family members have demonstrated little interest in my work or achievements in this arena. This has been very hard for me to accept emotionally and something that I cannot change, after many attempts to engage them. However, this is rather common in families of homicide loss. As a result, I feel in my heart that my small friends are like a true family.

As for loss of friends as a consequence of the homicide, I can't recall any true relationships being lost on this topic. If I did, they were relationships of little consequence anyway.

*

KIMBERLY HAWKS
Kimberly was 9 when her father Charles
died at age 32 in a car accident

I look back at my dad's passing now, twenty years later, and I feel that more of my relationships were affected than what I might have felt in the past. I look at two failed marriages and a close boyfriend whom I lost, and now I can see more of that impact now looking back. But when I was going through these relationship challenges, I didn't connect it to the loss of my dad at a young age and having my world get torn apart.

In terms of my relationship with my mother and with my siblings, all have been impacted greatly, and mostly for the worst. My relationship with my mother has improved throughout the years and we have become close. I'm still not as close to the rest of my siblings as I once was before the accident. And the biggest impact of them all is that my mother remarried and our stepfather treated us poorly and was often abusive. So the impact was felt many ways in my life.

*

VICKI HECKROTH
Vicki was 5 when her mother Bonnie
died at age 27 in an auto accident

The relationship impacted the most severely by my mother's death was the relationship between my father and myself. His life continued on with his new wife and daughter, while my life stood still. All of a sudden my own mother was gone, I had this new woman in my life that I was to call "mom," and a new little sister who took my place as Daddy's baby girl. No more cuddling on the couch at night waiting for mom to come home from work, no more close ties at all. So in a sense I lost both of my parents at that time. I didn't feel very special any longer.

\*

TERESA HERRING
Teresa was 47 when her father Burton
died at age 65 from brain cancer

The loss of my father caused a strain between my sister and I. We made the choice to grieve our father's death very differently. I felt abandoned by her during the time of our loss. She didn't draw close to me but choose to reach out to my aunt and my father's other family. In fact to this day we haven't talked about the situation surrounding his death, the funeral or any aspect of the loss. I think she managed to get closure with him and he, at the end, spent quality time with her. He choose not to give me that time. She had a very different relationship with him in many ways. It was harder for me to love and be forgiving of the man who abandoned us. I felt some sense of loyalty to my mother and felt it would hurt her if I chose to attend my father's funeral. Perhaps he had only abandoned me and she hadn't felt the same about him. My sister and I are working on building a stronger relationship now. She still has a relationship with my father's other family and I would be lying if I said it didn't hurt my feelings.

\*

BROOKE NINNI MATTHEWS
Brooke was 38 when her mother JoAnne
died at age 57 from cardiac arrhythmia

None, after I lost my mother. It wasn't until six months after my mother's passing, when I lost my only brother to murder that my losses impacted relationships.

\*

RUTH PAPALAS
Ruth was 41 when her father David
died at age 62 of a heart attack

My family's relationships were positively impacted. We spend more time together. We finally realize that anyone of us could be taken at any minute. We realize we are fortunate to still have Mom. If Mom wants or needs anything, we band together to make sure she has what she needs. We plan more time together. When we are together and then part, we part with an "I love you" and a hug. Friends are still very important, but family comes first.

\*

MARY LEE ROBINSON
Mary Lee was 56 when her father Pat
died at age 82 of a massive cerebral hemorrhage

I find my mother leans on me a lot now that Dad is gone. Then again, she is becoming elderly and there is some of that role reversal taking place. At the same time, she can't abide the idea of taking my advice, even when she asks my opinion. It's a hard time and a hard place for both of us. I do the best I can to navigate the last days of our earthly relationship as peaceably as I can. I know better than to take them for granted.

\*

PATTI SULLIVAN
Patti was 14 when her father Alfred
died at age 61 from a heart attack

My relationship with myself was impacted the most. I was at a loss for ten years. In my adulthood I was at a loss. I longed for my daddy so many times. If only he were here; I needed both of my parents, yet I had no one.

\*

JUDY TAYLOR
Judy was 55 when her mum Shirley
died at age 78 from a stroke

Everyone processes loss in their own way. In my experience the grief journey has strengthened many of my relationships through a necessity to open my heart and express myself. In the same way, this journey has highlighted relationships that were never strong and the necessity to accept this reality and let go has been heartbreaking for me.

\*

HEATHER WALLACE-REY
Heather was 40 when her father John
died suddenly at age 71 of a massive heart attack

Many years ago when my parents split up, it seemed to bring all five of my siblings and I much closer together. However with the passing of our father, for the first two years, it seemed to me that a number of us pushed each other away. One of my sisters and I both actually physically moved away in opposite directions, which is really the polar opposite of what one might guess would happen. I cannot and would not begin to speak for the five of them but in my mind we were emotionally very far apart from one another for a long time.

I think when you have five siblings and everyone is processing their loss in their own ways, on their own time, it becomes not only difficult but in some way excruciatingly painful to talk to those around you who are experiencing that very same loss. It occurs to me that no one really wants to cry or vent about their problems if the listener or support person has the very same problems. The five people in the world who had always, in some way, shape or form, been "my support people" were suddenly all over the map physically and emotionally. It seemed to me as if we all needed to go our own way in order to get through our mutual loss.

I know it is difficult for some of my siblings to read anything I've written about my loss, because it's their loss too. Frankly, I don't know that I would ever want to read anything they wrote about the loss of our father if the roles were reversed. However as time passes, it has gotten better. This year has gotten progressively better and we have been able to mend some fences and even talk a little about our dad with one another.

While I believe it is probably the relationship with my siblings that has been the most severely impacted by our mutual loss, I also know that the relationship I have with those other five people is the kind of relationship that has and will continue to withstand anything that comes our way. Both of our parents raised all six of us to take care of each other and of those around us. My dad was famous for his, "If people need your help, you help them," quote.

Being raised by my parents has given me faith, even in our very worst moments, that five of the greatest gifts I could ever ask for in life are the five people who I was raised with. And while I do believe that our relationship has been impacted by our loss, what I will always remember most is one moment: at my father's memorial service, the six of us walked in together, - myself and my five siblings - two by two, arm in arm: a loving reminder to all who were there of the unbreakable team that my parents built.

*

CHAPTER TWELVE

# THE FAITH

*Love is the only law capable*
*of transforming grief into hope.*
LYNDA CHELDELIN FELL

Grief has far-reaching effects in most areas of our life. Whether we're raised with faith or learn it later in life, loss can test our beliefs like nothing else. For some, our faith can deepen as it becomes a safe haven for our sorrow. For others, it can be a source of disappointment, leading to fractured beliefs. One commonality among the bereaved is that faith is often altered one way or the other.

*

SOPHIE BLOWERS
Sophie was 50 when her mother Amy
died at age 79 of internal bleeding

No, I can honestly say that in the long run my faith has remained the same. I questioned, I cried, I occasionally got angry, but I never really waivered. I am grateful for the fact that deep down I had a personal belief to lean on.

*

CHRISTINE DUMINIAK
Christine was 57 when her mother Ann
died at age 86 from an abdominal aortic aneurysm

My faith was extremely instrumental for my being able to quickly reinvest in life again. I found praying to God, asking Him to replace my heart's sorrow with His joy, helped tremendously in my healing. Part of God's help included my receiving comforting afterlife signs, yet this is rarely discussed in our churches. I believe talking about and recognizing that this spiritual phenomena exists would be one more important factor in aiding one's faith and healing.

*

WENDY EVANS
Wendy was 14 when her father Dwight
died at age 32 in a plane crash

Immediately following the death of my father I was young and attending church at time. Most of the church visits were with my dad. I had strong faith at that time and more coaches and support people from the church.

*

BONNIE FORSHEY
Bonnie was an infant when her father Andrew
died at age 41 from a cerebral hemorrhage
Bonnie was 60 when her mother Doris
died at age 81 from colon cancer

Yes it has impacted my faith. I just cannot understand how a loving god can allow people to suffer. My mother was a very religious woman. She prayed every day and thought that she would be cured.

\*

SKIP FRANKLIN
Skip was 41 when his mother Dianne
died at age 63 from a series of physical issues

My faith has not changed, it is really the rock of my existence. I have a lot of faith and human events, whether positive or negative, usually only result in increased faith. I do think it helped that I had already faced a lot of death. I don't really equate human death with spiritual being or spiritual identity. My sense of life is great. And I think some of my own near-death experiences served to strengthen that. But I have seen with my friends a total loss of faith after the passing of one of their parents. So I know it is very common and I certainly do not judge them. I can totally understand why.

\*

DONNA GORE
Donna was 26 when her father Donald
died by homicide in 1980

I do not consider myself a religious person or a person of strong faith, perhaps because I have had far too many trials in my life to question why and the presence of God. However, I do believe in God and think of myself as more of a spiritual person. Yes, the homicide loss definitely made me question even further the presence of God. However, I have come to realize over time, that I have been given many gifts to utilize as a result of such a loss. Therefore, I have faith that God is indeed watching over me and guiding my path.

\*

KIMBERLY HAWKS
Kimberly was 9 when her father Charles
died at age 32 in a car accident

The short answer is yes. My journey of faith has been a back-and-forth adventure. Initially my faith was tested, but grew stronger as I entered my teens. It then drifted a bit in adulthood, but again came back strong and today my faith is stronger than ever. I think both extremes in this pendulum swing were directly impacted by the loss of my dad. Ultimately, it solidified my faith that God was my Father and the only one who could fill that deep void inside me. I'm not sure this would be as strong today without the loss of my human dad. So lots of impact.

\*

VICKI HECKROTH
Vicki was 5 when her mother Bonnie
died at age 27 in an auto accident

When my mother passed, we went from being devout Catholic to not going to church, to becoming Lutheran like my new mom, and then becoming Jehovah's Witnesses. I now belong to the First Christian Church where I am just considered a Christian. I could not understand why God would let my mother sleep so long, and then as I got older could not understand how he could take her from me at such a young age. I both wanted and needed my mother much.

\*

TERESA HERRING
Teresa was 47 when her father Burton
died at age 65 from brain cancer

I never was one to use faith in any form for grieving. I believe it is because I was forced as a child and teenager to go to church which causes me to feel unconnected to religion. I believe in God but I feel like my father should have asked me for forgiveness also. I believe I need to forgive my father in order to move forward and release all this anger. I know it is not good for me to be angry but I am not at that point just yet.

\*

BROOKE NINNI MATTHEWS
Brooke was 38 when her mother JoAnne
died at age 57 from cardiac arrhythmia

Once again, my faith was not an issue until six months after my mother's passing, when I lost my only brother to murder. I used to believe you had to have a religion, but I don't believe that to be true anymore. I started studying and learning more about the afterlife and spirit world. I believe there is life after death, or shall I say there is no such thing as death. I believe we shed our physical bodies, our soul lives on in a higher dimension, each soul vibrates at a different level, and there is no hell. We are all children of God, he is in all of us, and he loves us all, therefore, I don't believe he would send us to a place like hell. I understand everyone has their own religion and belief, this is just mine.

\*

RUTH PAPALAS
Ruth was 41 when her father David
died at age 62 of a heart attack

My dad was a Christian man. He went to church every time the doors were open. My faith is stronger because I know Dad is in heaven and I want to see him again one day.

\*

MARY LEE ROBINSON
Mary Lee was 56 when her father Pat
died at age 82 of a massive cerebral hemorrhage

Dad's influence as a leader of the church and a man who walked the walk set a great example for me to follow. He leaned on his faith to cope with adversity.

*

PATTI SULLIVAN
Patti was 14 when her father Alfred
died at age 61 from a heart attack

Age has impacted my faith. The "faithful" have embarrassed themselves by their behavior.

*

JUDY TAYLOR
Judy was 55 when her mum Shirley
died at age 78 from a stroke

My faith and beliefs were tested to the core as the raw and confronting impact of death presented in my life. My mum and I had strong spiritual beliefs which we shared and discussed. However in my darkest moments I found it difficult to connect as my grief consumed me. Through my writing and also following practices that work for me, I have come home to my heart and found my faith and beliefs are stronger than ever.

*

HEATHER WALLACE-REY
Heather was 40 when her father John
died suddenly at age 71 of a massive heart attack

I have always considered myself to be a very faithful, prayerful person. I grew up as a church kid, and have worked in ministry for almost all of my adult life and cannot remember a time when I didn't believe in God. My struggle with my faith since my father died has not been about whether or not I believe in God, but rather what to do with a God that refuses the one miracle you really need and are praying for. I should know better than to bargain with God, but I have always held a strong belief that God CAN make miracles happen, and yet these miracles were not sent to save my dad's life that day, which left me with some serious questions. I know how imperfect I am, but there are times (this being a stellar example) where I want to believe in a God that doesn't simply answer my prayers, but actually answers my prayers in the way I see fit. Sometimes I want to believe in a God that gives me what I am praying for; a God that gives me what I want. And then I remember: that's not God... that's Santa Claus.

It is difficult to believe in a God that left me with a broken, shattered life where I believe a strong faith used to be. I have always been a little bit of a "doubting Thomas" but, at least for a while, loss and grief really threw my faith for a loop that I never knew previously existed; even as a doubter.

I have been really, really angry with God, although I know God is more than capable of dealing with my anger. For a while, I was so angry with God that I refused to talk to God. I stopped praying. I continued teaching Sunday school but I added in phrases like "what our church believes is...." instead of phrasing things as I would usually, which include some of the things I personally believe. I wasn't sure what I believed anymore. I wasn't sure IF I believed anymore. I did not WANT to believe in a God that would let my dad die without giving me the chance to say goodbye. And I still have a clipboard long list of questions for God on this subject for some time in the future.

Overall, it took me the better part of three years to get to a place where I can be okay with being angry with God, and not being able to understand God's plan, but understanding that I can still have a strong faith, despite my anger. I continue to hope that my faith will be strengthened through sharing my story and listening to the stories of others.

*

I walked a mile with Pleasure;
She chatted all the way.
But left me none the wiser
for all she had to say.

I walked a mile with Sorrow;
And ne'er a word said she.
But, oh! The things I
learned from her,
when Sorrow walked with me.
ROBERT BROWNING HAMILTON

*

CHAPTER THIRTEEN

# OUR HEALTH

*Health is a state of complete physical, mental, and social well-being,*
*and not merely the absence of disease or infirmity.*
WORLD HEALTH ORGANIZATION

As our anatomical and physiological systems work in tandem with our emotional well-being, when one part of our body is stressed, other parts become compromised. Has your grief affected your physical health?

\*

SOPHIE BLOWERS
Sophie was 50 when her mother Amy
died at age 79 of internal bleeding

I am a very gregarious person. I am big in my movements, I laugh loud, and I make direct eye contact. Since Mom has died, I have struggled being me. I have become a little withdrawn, preferring to be alone on my laptop. I have been less likely to volunteer for things. I am tired much of the time. The funny thing is that I had not realized this until this moment, when answering this question. My initial thought was, "Nope, no difference in my health." Then I stopped and actually thought about it. It is so easy to ignore the nuances of life. It is the small things that change us over time, the no longer laughing as loud or as hard. I think I will make the choice to laugh today, even if it is a little forced. Maybe tomorrow it won't be.

*

CHRISTINE DUMINIAK
Christine was 57 when her mother Ann
died at age 86 from an abdominal aortic aneurysm

I have not noticed a change in my physical health since my loss. I believe that is because of my acceptance of the loss, as well as my faith knowing that my loved one is like an angel on my shoulder now. I also believed that my loved one and God wanted me to be happy again, so I have tried to honor that.

*

WENDY EVANS
Wendy was 14 when her father Dwight
died at age 32 in a plane crash

At fourteen, the physical changes to one's body is overwhelming just because of normal changes due to hormones. I don't recall any negative or positive changes in my health that could be directly tied to the death event.

*

BONNIE FORSHEY
Bonnie was an infant when her father Andrew
died at age 41 from a cerebral hemorrhage
Bonnie was 60 when her mother Doris
died at age 81 from colon cancer

My health has declined. I have a lot of autoimmune diseases now. It seems like one thing after another. I am depressed and in a lot of pain. I have rheumatoid arthritis, osteoarthritis, lupus, diabetes, chronic fatigue syndrome and more.

\*

SKIP FRANKLIN
Skip was 41 when his mother Dianne
died at age 63 from a series of physical issues

I really don't think it affected my physical health per se. But I can see how that could happen to people. In my own experience I had dealt with several deaths and even some near-death situations of my own. This ultimately had a very positive effect on me. It would be easy to describe it as a "detachment" from the human condition, but I would like to describe it as an elevation to a different manifestation of life, a life not dependent upon blood circulating and brain cells firing. A life that draws from a higher source and feeds on a divine Spirit. It is very different from my view of twenty years ago. It is not a theory or a commitment, it is really a feeling. A deep feeling. And one that has been proved on several occasions. That my life is not my own. God is my life.

\*

DONNA GORE
Donna was 26 when her father Donald
died by homicide in 1980

Despite all of my surgeries, my general health has always been very good. I did go through several years of counseling for many of the events in my life, including the homicide. I would say that the greatest impact resulting from homicide loss was my vulnerability, (part of my emotional health) which was altered forever after the homicide. As a person with a disability, I have always felt more physically vulnerable. I can't run away or kick a perpetrator where it hurts to make an escape. The homicide just made that vulnerability more heightened which I resent to this day.

*

KIMBERLY HAWKS
Kimberly was 9 when her father Charles
died at age 32 in a car accident

Physically, I think some of my eating disorders could be traced back to my loss. The first was not eating enough and trying to be a skinny teen and not showing my female developments. Later, after having children, my eating disorders went the other way and I found myself more than one hundred pounds overweight.

Psychologically, I think some of the horrors of that car accident still haunt me in my dreams and affect the trauma levels in my daily experience. Over time and through faith, I think some of this has been softened and healed, but my human experience to date has definitely been impacted. And the psychological and emotional issues have probably affected my health in ways I don't realize. But fortunately, the increase in my faith and the wisdom and self-knowledge that I have gained in dealing with this has had an equally big impact for the good.

*

VICKI HECKROTH
Vicki was 5 when her mother Bonnie
died at age 27 in an auto accident

My self-esteem went way downhill. If someone touched me, I would cringe because I thought my ugliness would rub off on them. I thought I was the most disgusting and ugly person there was. I hated my bright red hair and got teased so much because of it, and also because my last name was Handy. So although my mother's death did not affect my physical health, it did affect my mental health.

\*

## TERESA HERRING
Teresa was 47 when her father Burton
died at age 65 from brain cancer

I became very depressed by the situation around the loss of my father, more so than the actual death of him. I was very disappointed and hurt by the actions of several family members. I was disappointed that no one reached out to help me in the mourning process, to check on me or walk with me through it. I think depression affects my health every day. It has also become clear during the course of this writing that anger has a lot to do with it too. Some days are overwhelming still to this day, and I have to take a break and spend the day in tears and bed. I know I would be better if I forgave my father and let the anger go. I know that will happen someday, but for today I am not ready to do either of those things. I just have to try to be kind to my body and mind and realize that it will come in time.

\*

## BROOKE NINNI MATTHEWS
Brooke was 38 when her mother JoAnne
died at age 57 from cardiac arrhythmia

I have not experienced a change in my physical health after my mother's passing, but my daughter did. She suffered from depression and extreme anxiety to the point where she had to be admitted into a child's psychiatric unit for a week.

\*

## RUTH PAPALAS
Ruth was 41 when her father David
died at age 62 of a heart attack

I was unfortunately on an upward swing of weight gain even before Dad died. After he died, I found myself eating more and more. I would eat the things Dad loved and think of my dad. I can't explain what one had to do with the other. Anyway, I ended up having a gastric bypass three to four years after he died. Because he had a heart attack, I never miss my annual physical exams, blood work, EKG, etc. I see, in my brothers especially, the health issues that we have to deal with that comes from Dad's side of the family.

*

PATTI SULLIVAN
Patti was 14 when her father Alfred
died at age 61 from a heart attack

I think when my dad died I became very sad. I tried drugs and drinking, I didn't care. That affected me in a negative way and I lost weight because I quit eating.

*

JUDY TAYLOR
Judy was 55 when her mum Shirley
died at age 78 from a stroke

Throughout my grieving my health has been good when I allowed myself to express my feelings. At the times when I have been in denial of the reality of my mum's death, when I kept busy as a distraction and soldiered on then my health issues presented. It is amazing how our bodies let us know when we are not taking care of ourselves. I learned that nurturing myself and taking care of my physical health are an important part of the grieving process for me.

*

HEATHER WALLACE-REY
Heather was 40 when her father John
died suddenly at age 71 of a massive heart attack

At the beginning of my third year of loss, I went to the doctor because I thought I was having a heart attack. I had massive chest and arm pain and was having trouble breathing. My doctor did an EKG and a few other tests. When the results came in, my doctor came into the examining room with one thing to say, "There's nothing wrong with your heart. So tell me what's going on with your life."

As the tears and stress poured out of me that day, I discussed with my physician how stress can (and was doing its best to) ruin my physical health. It was at that time that I finally agreed to try antidepressants. If this is a part of your story, I want you to know that my struggle with antidepressants went a little like this, starting two weeks after I agreed to try them:

Me: How do I know if this drug is helping?

Nurse: How are you feeling?

Me: I don't really know. I don't really feel anything.

Nurse: What do you mean when you say "you don't feel anything?"

Me: Am I supposed to not care about a single thing? Because, if so, this drug is TOTALLY working. I don't care if I go to work.

Nurse: Did you go to work?

Me: Yes. But who cares?

Nurse: Let me talk with the doctor and get back to you.

Me: I also don't care about whether or not my kids go to school, or if the dogs are fed, or if anyone eats dinner, of if anyone in my whole house has clean clothes to wear, or if people are mad at me. I don't care about anything. Does that mean this drug is working?

Nurse: When is a good time to call you back?

Me: Who cares?

Nurse: Yes, this might not be the right drug for you.

This definitely wasn't the right drug for me. If this is a part of your story, I want you to know this: the antidepressants didn't work the first time. In fact, it took four rounds in order to find the right combination of antidepressants for my body.

For some people (including me) the antidepressants do work. They don't for everyone. Having to take antidepressants doesn't make you crazy. It means you need something to get you a little further along in the grief process. Needing help (even pharmaceutical help) is nothing to be ashamed of. Not getting the help you need is the part of grief that needs to be avoided.

Since that day in the doctor's office, I have decided that since each one of us has a limited amount of heartbeats left in our lives, I would really like to spend those limited heartbeats with the people I love and doing the things I love to do. Going back to regularly exercising has helped immensely in the way I feel.

*

CHAPTER FOURTEEN

# THE QUIET

*Heavy hearts, like heavy clouds in the sky,*
*are best relieved by the letting go of a little water.*
ANTOINE RIVAROL

The void left in our parent's absence can fill our days and nights. When our minds are free from distractions there is a moment when sorrow fills that void, threatening to overtake us, unleashing the torrent of tears. For some, that moment happens during the day, for others it comes at night. What time is hardest for you?

*

SOPHIE BLOWERS
Sophie was 50 when her mother Amy
died at age 79 of internal bleeding

Mornings and evenings are both hard for totally different reasons. Mom was a morning person. Every morning without fail, I would see her at the kitchen table in her bathrobe and slippers, sipping coffee. Chock full o'Nuts... always. We would have a cup of coffee or four and talk about the day, the weather, the kids...it did not matter. It was our time. Evenings are hard because during the initial caregiving stage, right after mom's stroke, my sister and I would get mom tucked in bed and we would sit on the front porch with a large vodka. We would stare at each other for a few minutes, trying to comprehend the events of the day, and let me assure you, every day caring for a stroke patient has events of some sort. My sister and I would slowly begin to talk about the day, the weather, Mom… it did not matter. It was our time. I miss the companionship of both of these women on a daily basis. This shows that even in the darkest of times, there is something beautiful and it somehow always revolves around love.

*

CHRISTINE DUMINIAK
Christine was 57 when her mother Ann
died at age 86 from an abdominal aortic aneurysm

The hardest part of the day was anytime I wanted to call my mother and tell her something, so it could be any time of the day or night. It was a sad reminder that I could no longer share things with her. It has gotten better over time, as my husband and my sister have helped to fill that void. But a very important part of my healing was because my best friend is a highly regarded Christian spiritual medium, so I have benefited tremendously by getting to "talk" to my mother through my best friend's spiritual gift. So in my case it is almost like my mother is just a phone call away.

*

WENDY EVANS
Wendy was 14 when her father Dwight
died at age 32 in a plane crash

I am struggling to remember that far back. I believe it was at night or the evening. Interrupted sleep or lack of sleep as I recall. Going to school was a challenge due to the early reporting time.

148

\*

SKIP FRANKLIN
Skip was 41 when his mother Dianne
died at age 63 from a series of physical issues

I really don't have a hardest time of day. I think with me it is triggered more by human events that I witness: A son having a coffee at Starbucks with his mom. A boy playing cards with his mother on the airplane. I played a zillion hands of Gin Rummy with my mom and it would be fun to get together, grab a cup of coffee and play some hands of Gin. That would be beyond awesome!

\*

KIMBERLY HAWKS
Kimberly was 9 when her father Charles
died at age 32 in a car accident

Good question. Probably at night when I dream. I often have challenges during the sleeping hours. I would say that is when I am most affected.

\*

VICKI HECKROTH
Vicki was 5 when her mother Bonnie
died at age 27 in an auto accident

The hardest part of the day for me was nighttime. I was afraid to go to sleep because I had been told my mother was sleeping until Jesus woke her up. I was afraid that if I went to sleep, I also would need Jesus to wake me up and that they would put me in a pretty box and cover me up with dirt like they did my mommy.

*

TERESA HERRING
Teresa was 47 when her father Burton
died at age 65 from brain cancer

I don't think about him much, but if I had to pick a time I think night is the hardest for me and of course when a depression sets in. The inner voice always says: he left you, he didn't love you, and he chose his other family over you. I have chased the father figure all my life. I tried to love all forms of men in the process; tall, skinny, short, fat, different nationalities, all the while thinking maybe this one will love me. Missing my father's love has also led me to be in both physically and emotionally abusive relationships where a small part of me felt I deserved it. Seeking the love of a father is an elusive dream that I don't think or, should I say I know, I will never find. Learning to accept that is where I stand in my grief today.


*

BROOKE NINNI MATTHEWS
Brooke was 38 when her mother JoAnne
died at age 57 from cardiac arrhythmia

I struggled most during daytime after losing my mom. My mom and I would put my children on the bus and then she and I would spend the day out. We would do breakfast, then do some shopping and then lunch, and then more shopping. We also did a lot of day trips in the summertime with my children and my nephew.

*

RUTH PAPALAS
Ruth was 41 when her father David
died at age 62 of a heart attack

At first it was when I tried to go to sleep. My head would start racing and I would think of all the "woulda, coulda, shouldas." I would cry myself to sleep. I started taking a sleeping pill to fall asleep but not to excess. I just needed some sleep. Later on the hardest time was dinnertime at Mom's. I did not realize how many evenings I took for granted being at Mom and Dad's for dinner. Once Mom started cooking again several weeks later, it didn't seem right to enjoy meals that Dad loved. It has been years, so I'm able to enjoy those meals again without feeling a giant sense of "this was Dad's favorite...and he's not here." It's been seventeen years now. I still miss Dad but now I can fall sleep without thinking about Dad and having any regrets.

Now, I miss Dad more at events that he should have been at such as graduations, weddings, births and other deaths (his beloved brother). I still cry when there's a memorial table at one of these events and my dad's picture is there because he isn't.

*

MARY LEE ROBINSON
Mary Lee was 56 when her father Pat
died at age 82 of a massive cerebral hemorrhage

My mother used to call me in the morning to see if I was coming to visit, and then again at 7 p.m. to talk and say goodnight. I miss those calls.

*

PATTI SULLIVAN
Patti was 14 when her father Alfred
died at age 61 from a heart attack

I grieved all day, every day for ten years. I loved my dad with everything I am. I will always love him. He was wonderful to me, even at his sickest times. Super ball Daddy, let's play!!! I just bought two of them, for old times' sake.

\*

JUDY TAYLOR
Judy was 55 when her mum Shirley
died at age 78 from a stroke

From memory there was no particular time of day that was specifically hard. There were times I sat in shock, disbelief, and the raw reality of my mum never walking up my pathway again. At other times I felt her presence so strongly that I celebrated the connection we still had. I found in the first six months after Mum's death that I sat in silence in bed most nights allowing my feelings to flow, and flow they did. Over times I set the intention to stay connected with her and allowed myself time to make a cup of tea and sit and chat to her, just like we had when she was living. I also wrote to her to talk about my feelings and visited places she loved and places we both loved. The more I practiced this the stronger the connection. This has and continues to sustain me today. It is a beautiful way for us to connect.

\*

ALEXIS VON UTTER
Alexis was 12 when her father Marc
died at age 57 from lung cancer complications

My dad used to pick me up right after school and we would go to the grocery store together. We would go home. I would get ready for whatever sport I had that season, we would pick up my brother from the metro, and then go to practice. My dad would coach the practice and then afterwards we would go home. I would get ready for bed, I would then do my homework while my dad would get dinner ready, and then we would eat as a family. After that we would watch TV and have some dessert and then off to bed. Now I don't have that routine and for me it is hard to get stuff done without it being planned out.

*

HEATHER WALLACE-REY
Heather was 40 when her father John
died suddenly at age 71 of a massive heart attack

For probably about a month after my father died, I had one moment every morning when I was somewhere between asleep and waking. I was not yet fully awake, so my body and my brain had forgotten that I had lost someone. For those few seconds, I had that happy, relaxed moment when the sun was shining through the window onto my face, and I had one moment of easy breathing, and even a little contented sigh. After my brain and body became fully awake, I then had a really awful moment when I realized that this wasn't just a nightmare. This was real. It really happened. That was the awful moment when I was awake enough to remember that this searing pain through my heart was now my new normal.

A month or so after my dad's death, I lost that initial moment of happy contented sighing, and knew immediately when I woke up that my father was gone. That was really difficult. I think just knowing that my brain, even in the moments from sleeping to waking, had resigned and accepted that my dad was gone made that month the most difficult. I wanted so badly to hang on to that initial waking up moment when I could just breathe easily and be contented and feel that all was right with the world.

*

The emotions of grief are universal,
but the experience of grief is not.
EMILY BARNHARDT

*

# CHAPTER FIFTEEN

# OUR FEAR

*The oldest and strongest emotion of mankind is fear,*
*and the oldest and strongest kind of fear is fear of the unknown.*
H. P. LOVECRAFT

Fear can cut like a knife and immobilize us like a straitjacket. It whispers to us that our lives will never be the same, our misfortunes will manifest themselves again, and that we are helpless. How do we control our fear, so it doesn't control us?

\*

SOPHIE BLOWERS
Sophie was 50 when her mother Amy
died at age 79 of internal bleeding

I am afraid of not recovering completely. I know I will never be the same, but what if I lose the parts of me I liked? What if the hurt drives me to live in a safe place and I never take risks again? I guess I am terrified of not taking anything away from this loss; of not finding some purpose in all of the pain.

*

### CHRISTINE DUMINIAK
Christine was 57 when her mother Ann
died at age 86 from an abdominal aortic aneurysm

From time to time as people I know have lost their spouses, I tend to imagine what would life be without my own husband. However, I believe that with God's help, that when this happens, that I will eventually be okay. God has always helped me in the past and I have always been able to get through every hardship and challenge by holding God and Jesus' hand.

*

### WENDY EVANS
Wendy was 14 when her father Dwight
died at age 32 in a plane crash

I was very afraid of what would become of my brothers and me. After our father died our mom went into a deep depression that prevented her from being available for us. It was frightening to think about if we could go to college, did we have funds to go to college, what were we expected to do after high school.

*

### BONNIE FORSHEY
Bonnie was an infant when her father Andrew
died at age 41 from a cerebral hemorrhage
Bonnie was 60 when her mother Doris
died at age 81 from colon cancer

I fear colon cancer. It took my mother's life and runs in our family.

*

SKIP FRANKLIN
Skip was 41 when his mother Dianne
died at age 63 from a series of physical issues

"Don't die with your music still inside you," was Dr. Wayne Dyer's message in the film, *The Shift*. My mom was active and accomplished a lot, but I can't help but have the feeling that she died with the music still inside. And that would be my greatest fear as well. I'd like to avoid that.

*

DONNA GORE
Donna was 26 when her father Donald
died by homicide in 1980

I think the fear I experience stems from feeling vulnerable in the aftermath of homicide loss. I feel vulnerable because of my physical disabilities. I simply can't get away from an attacker.

*

KIMBERLY HAWKS
Kimberly was 9 when her father Charles
died at age 32 in a car accident

I think the experience has made me more fearless as much as it made me more fearful. I definitely received a huge wake-up call at the early age of nine about loss and mortality, and this affected me in both directions. Was I ever afraid that I might die young like my father? Perhaps. But it wasn't necessarily a fear. I think there are times that I'm afraid to be alone and feel unprotected or vulnerable. But there are other times that I prefer to be alone and am oblivious to danger. I think my business partner would answer this question much differently. He would say I am afraid of success, afraid of fully reaching my potential and realizing the full benefit of my mission and music and ministry. Afraid to let my light shine and really go for it. He might be right. But I think everyone struggles with this, whether they lost their father at age nine or not. But it would be hard to argue that my daddy's death didn't play a role in my struggle. And that some of my fears and doubts could be traced back to having my life shattered by the death of my daddy when I was nine.

*

VICKI HECKROTH
Vicki was 5 when her mother Bonnie
died at age 27 in an auto accident

I am most afraid of having my girls go through some of the same things I did when the time comes for me to go to Heaven. I was and still am such a wreck at times that I fear they will be the same. I also fear that after I am gone, my family will let the few memories of my mom die with me. I fear that she will be forgotten.

*

TERESA HERRING
Teresa was 47 when her father Burton
died at age 65 from brain cancer

I fear my father never loved me; even at the end he failed to help me heal the wounds he caused. My father had the opportunity to at least attempt to heal the childhood wounds, yet he never did. It wasn't because he didn't have time; in fact I spent several hours with him prior to his death. I fear I will never be able to accept that he didn't love me. I fear I will never be able to understand why. Why did he reach out to every child except me? What was it about me? I fear I won't be able to accept and move past the anger. He is not here; the chapter with him is closed. He can't help or hurt me anymore. I have been stuck in anger for too long. He really is not worth spending so much energy on. I would like to say that he was incapable of being a good father and of showing love, but that is not true. He is the father of four other children. I am beginning to think anger is where I will be stuck forever.

158

*

BROOKE NINNI MATTHEWS
Brooke was 38 when her mother JoAnne
died at age 57 from cardiac arrhythmia

I really fear of what would happen to my children and how they would react to my passing, especially my daughter. She struggled so much with losing my mom, so I can't imagine what she will be like when I pass away.

*

RUTH PAPALAS
Ruth was 41 when her father David
died at age 62 of a heart attack

Dying at or before age sixty-two.

*

PATTI SULLIVAN
Patti was 14 when her father Alfred
died at age 61 from a heart attack

That I have to die and not see my family.

*

JUDY TAYLOR
Judy was 55 when her mum Shirley
died at age 78 from a stroke

In the beginning the pain was so raw, and many times I feared I would never get over it. As a result of my dedication to staying connected through my writing and other practices, I have found the pain has reduced dramatically. I still have moments when the reality that she is not here physically can take me completely by surprise, and the pain can be as intense as in the early days. At these times I allow my feelings to flow and embrace whatever emotion presents. This is part of my own personal healing process.

*

ALEXIS VON UTTER
Alexis was 12 when her father Marc
died at age 57 from lung cancer complications

I am most afraid of getting into college. My dad always helped me with homework and getting good grades and now that I don't have his support, I don't really know what to do and how to study and do my homework. My biggest fear is what am I going to be in my future, because it is fast approaching.

*

HEATHER WALLACE-REY
Heather was 40 when her father John
died suddenly at age 71 of a massive heart attack

I think my biggest fears since the death of my father have centered around anything that will leave permanent regret in my heart or in the hearts of others if I were to die today, or if someone else I loved or cared about were to die today. Living with the regret of not being able to say goodbye to my dad, and knowing that the last thing I said to my dad was two weeks before his death and wasn't, "I love you," has made me come to very harsh terms with the limited number of heartbeats I have left. I am now ultra-aware of my own mortality, and it affects how I live.

While this might seem like a positive thing, and sometimes it is, it has also taken some negative turns because I have found myself clinging extremely tightly to friends, relatives and people I love. I am very aware that this clinging is not necessarily about having someone to hold on to, but much of it is about clinging to other people because I am so afraid of THEIR mortality. Over the past three and a half years, this fear has made me feel like I am drowning and, much like any drowning person, I look around and clutch too tightly to anyone and everyone around me, which has sometimes threatened to take others "down with me."

Over time and with counseling, I am re-learning how to let go of things and loosen my grip on people so I don't feel the need to have a strangle-hold on everything and everyone around me. I have had to learn the hard way that life is promised to no one, and that there are many things about life that are out of our control. I certainly do not want to lose anyone else in my life to death, although logically I know that death is a part of life. More importantly, I do not want to lose anyone in my life because my own fear made me hold onto them too tightly, nor do I want to lose anyone else without saying what I need to say to them. I don't want anyone to leave without hearing me say how much I love and care about them. Closure has become infinitely important. I am learning that the only way to fix regret is to try to do better, or to do it differently, the next time.

*

Tears don't stop
with years.
EMILY BAIRD-LEVINE

*

# CHAPTER SIXTEEN

# OUR COMFORT

*Life is made up, not of great sacrifices or duties, but of little things,*
*in which smiles and kindness, and small obligations given habitually,*
*are what preserve the heart and secure comfort.*
HUMPHRY DAVY

Transition sometimes feels as if we have embarked on a foreign journey with no companion, compass, or light. Rather than fill our bag with necessities, we often seek to fill it with emotional items that bring us comfort as we find our way through the eye of the storm. What items or rituals bring you the most comfort?

*

SOPHIE BLOWERS
Sophie was 50 when her mother Amy
died at age 79 of internal bleeding

My family and my friends have all been fantastic, but there is always a feeling of having to be the strong one. The comforter. I never feel like I can truly just let go. This is ridiculous and I know people will scoff, but my greatest comfort comes from my dog. He give me the purest, most unconditional love I have ever experienced. He is easy to be around; I do not have to think or work at it. He is my companion, my cuddle buddy, and my reminder that

I am actually worthy of love and that it will not go away. I know he will never leave me by his choice...but then again...neither did Mom.

*

CHRISTINE DUMINIAK
Christine was 57 when her mother Ann
died at age 86 from an abdominal aortic aneurysm

Wearing my mother's wedding ring brings me a lot of comfort and I feel her presence around me when I do.

*

WENDY EVANS
Wendy was 14 when her father Dwight
died at age 32 in a plane crash

I think prayer and talking to my dad in my head brought me the most comfort. My brothers were there for me to protect and that gave me purpose and comfort.

*

BONNIE FORSHEY
Bonnie was an infant when her father Andrew
died at age 41 from a cerebral hemorrhage
Bonnie was 60 when her mother Doris
died at age 81 from colon cancer

I love to think back on our times together, and I love the pictures that I have of her.

\*

SKIP FRANKLIN
Skip was 41 when his mother Dianne
died at age 63 from a series of physical issues

I think in terms of my mom, what gives me the most comfort is seeing my dad being taken care of, and all of my siblings in a good place. I know that would be important for my mom. She would be very pleased to see how close we all are, with frequent communication. That gives me the most comfort.

\*

DONNA GORE
Donna was 26 when her father Donald
died by homicide in 1980

At this juncture, with the perspective I have after thirty-four years, I have comfort in the knowledge that I have evolved from devastation to being able to thrive, bringing comfort, knowledge, awareness and assistance to others in entirely different ways that I never thought possible! Particularly in the last five plus years, selected mentors such as the late Susan Murphy Milano, a homicide survivor, national advocate, champion of many cutting edge programs for those suffering intimate partner and family violence, Delilah Jones, President of Imagine Publicity.com and Monica Caison, Founder of the Cue Center for Missing Persons have given me opportunities and made an indelible mark on my life! All of these opportunities to raise awareness and act as a crime victim advocate bring me comfort by knowing that I'm making a difference.

*

KIMBERLY HAWKS
Kimberly was 9 when her father Charles
died at age 32 in a car accident

Spiritually what has brought me comfort is that losing a human daddy has brought me closer to my divine Father, God, and my relationship with Him. And this spiritual strength and comfort and peace has been life-changing. I don't know if I would be here today without that. I think this would be the main thing.

In terms of human comforts, good and bad, there have been times in my experience where food and alcohol played too big of a role in terms of both immediate comfort and filling the inner void. On the plus side has been my love of music and expressing my feelings through songwriting, singing and playing music. I think these have both healed me as well as those my music has touched. Dozens of fulfilling relationships have developed from both my music and my ministry that have been a great comfort for both givers and receivers. And even though I still experience those "moments" that we all go through, each year is becoming more fulfilling and empowering and comforting. I like where I am today. I feel like I've been through quite a journey to get here and I've come a long way.

*

VICKI HECKROTH
Vicki was 5 when her mother Bonnie
died at age 27 in an auto accident

It brings me comfort knowing that my mother is in Heaven watching over me. It comforts me to know that she is with two of my children, that she knows my triumphs and losses, and that she is always just the blink of an eye away. I talk to her often, asking for guidance in my life. I know she is always with me.

\*

TERESA HERRING
Teresa was 47 when her father Burton
died at age 65 from brain cancer

I don't have anything of my fathers. Not one single item. I bought myself a teddy bear from Build-A-Bear a few years back. I placed a recording of my voice in its foot. When pressed it says, "You were a good child, you are a good woman. I will always love and take care of you." It has been in my closet for a few years until the other night. I woke in the middle of the night, went to find it, played the recording and then took it back to bed with me. I feel I needed it while going through this writing process and it has become a source of comfort. I also have a picture of me at about age five that is my favorite. I look at it, look at my eyes and face, how small I am. How vulnerable my five-year-old self looks, and realize there is nothing that that beautiful child could do ever to not deserve love from both parents. She is unable to understand, cope or protect herself but yet she had to. She was learning things about love, life, family and feeling safe. All the same things I still feel today. That five-year-old self comforts me by knowing I would love and protect this small child at all costs and, in fact, today I am still fighting to keep her safe and alive.

I find comfort in knowing I have raised two healthy, loved and caring men who have become amazing parents to my grandchildren. I find comfort in knowing that even though I had no real positive parental involvement except my grandparents, I was able to change the cycle for my children. I made sure they were loved and never had to question how I felt about them or if they were wanted. I love them and they truly are my heart and make me very proud to be their mother.

\*

BROOKE NINNI MATTHEWS
Brooke was 38 when her mother JoAnne
died at age 57 from cardiac arrhythmia

This may sound a bit odd, but it brings me comfort knowing that my brother and mom are both reunited and together again.

\*

RUTH PAPALAS
Ruth was 41 when her father David
died at age 62 of a heart attack

Knowing that my dad is in heaven brings me the absolute most comfort. Beyond that, I have Dad's photos scattered about. After Dad died, I found a necklace in a catalog called a "memorial tear." I bought it and have worn it ever since. When the chain breaks, I just buy a new chain. I have several necklaces, yet this is the one I wear. I touch it several times a day and feel naked if I forget to put it on. It's my "touchstone."

\*

MARY LEE ROBINSON
Mary Lee was 56 when her father Pat
died at age 82 of a massive cerebral hemorrhage

I have many things that were my dad's, as well as some family things going back further. I still have a red and gray flannel robe that was a Christmas gift to him from my grandmother, his mother-in-law. She sewed it for him about fifty years ago. It's still in great shape, and I wear it now and then. I also have Dad's portrait on my living room wall, as I do my wedding picture with my husband. I sit and look at those and they always give me strength. My husband and my dad were Irish. My dad was also Scottish. I thoroughly enjoy Celtic events, music and movies. They make me feel connected to all who went before, and bore heavier burdens that I ever have. I also have the letter Dad wrote to me as I prepared to go off to college. I doubt that he knew I kept it. I reread it now and then. He was my hero. They all were my heroes. Thinking of my family, now mostly gone, helps me get things back into perspective.

*

PATTI SULLIVAN
Patti was 14 when her father Alfred
died at age 61 from a heart attack

Parades! Flags! My dad was a veteran and we always went to parades. We would go to a small town and lo and behold there would be a parade. Now I collect flags. My dad also loved children, and I do too. I have worked with kids my whole life and I still do!!

*

JUDY TAYLOR
Judy was 55 when her mum Shirley
died at age 78 from a stroke

Many things bring me comfort including writing to my mum, creating quiet time to chat to her in spirit whilst having a cup of tea or walking in nature, meditation, lighting candles, visiting places mum loved, visiting places mum and I both loved, hugging a shawl mum gifted me, wearing pieces of her clothing that suit me, spending time with her friends and so much more. I am often guided by my intuition when I need to create time to be with her.

*

ALEXIS VON UTTER
Alexis was 12 when her father Marc
died at age 57 from lung cancer complications

Comedy shows and music brings me comfort. Comedians always lift my spirit and make it better. They know how to make me laugh and bring me out of whatever is going on at that time.

*

HEATHER WALLACE-REY
Heather was 40 when her father John
died suddenly at age 71 of a massive heart attack

Grief and I have come a very long way in three and a half years. Shortly after my father's death, I had taken to wearing or holding onto his former possessions that I believe provided comfort. I had decided it was a good idea (during grief, I'm pretty sure the phrase "good idea" is all relative) to wear my dad's winter coat around in the middle of summer, mostly because it still smelled like him.

One of my least favorite moments - although still hilarious to my children (and throngs of other people who are certainly too dignified to either let this kind of thing happen to them or - at least to ever talk about it) was the moment when my youngest, now sixteen years-old, caught me sitting on the floor of my walk-in closet, sobbing while smelling my father's shoes. There are moments of lunacy that can never truly be recreated, like the moment when you hear your teenage son say to your husband, "Dad, do NOT go in there. She's sitting on the floor, smelling grandpa's shoes. Nothing good can come of this. Actually....Dad....do we have any Mike's Hard Lemonade? We might be able to get her to come out if we use that as an incentive." As moments of comfort go, I wish I could say I was one of those people who dealt with grief in a mature and dignified way, but that was never the case.

One of the more dignified ways that provided comfort to me during that time involved my dad's keys. My dad owned a bus company and collected (or hoarded) keys. For the renewal of my wedding vows, which my husband and I did in Mexico, I made a bouquet that included a few of my dad's keys tied with ribbons. It was comforting to have those keys with me as a symbol of his presence with us because, at our actual wedding, he was there to walk me down the aisle. I needed some part of him to be there for the vow renewal.

My dad became a Buddhist a few years before his death and, as such, often spoke about coming back (reincarnation) as a butterfly or a cricket. For one summer after he died, I did extensive library research and designed and planted a butterfly garden to honor his memory. It wasn't just about the garden. Every time I felt exhausted by grief, or terribly sad or unproductive, I would go outside and plant something, or weed something or water something. The ability to be productive when I didn't feel like it brought so much comfort. An added benefit now is that we have a pretty garden and we look forward to butterflies every summer. When I see the butterflies each summer it is a comfort and a reminder that my dad is still very much with me.

*

*"There is no death, daughter.*
*People die only when we forget them,"*
*my mother explained, shortly before she left me.*
*"If you can remember me,*
*I will be with you always."*
ISABEL ALLENDE

*

# CHAPTER SEVENTEEN

# OUR SILVER LINING

*Even a small star shines in darkness.*
FINNISH PROVERB

In the earliest days following loss, the thought that anything good can come from our experience is beyond comprehension. Yet some say there are blessings in everything. Have you discovered a silver lining in your loss?

\*

SOPHIE BLOWERS
Sophie was 50 when her mother Amy
died at age 79 of internal bleeding

I have a much closer relationship with my sister. We have forged that kind of relationship that you see all the cute sayings on Facebook describe, you know the "my sister is my best friend... repost if you have a sister you just can't live without." Well, I really couldn't live without my sister, or at least I sure would not want to try. I don't know that there is anything that can elicit greater emotion than grieving together. Whether you are the griever, the support or both, the raw and powerful emotions can forge a bond like no other. My sister gets it when we talk about Mom, or the emotions. I don't have to explain, she just gets it.

\*

CHRISTINE DUMINIAK
Christine was 57 when her mother Ann
died at age 86 from an abdominal aortic aneurysm

Although I have always been close to my two sisters and consider them my friends, sharing the loss of our mother brought us even closer together. It helped me to really appreciate and value them in my life, and I believe they feel the same way too.

\*

BONNIE FORSHEY
Bonnie was an infant when her father Andrew
died at age 41 from a cerebral hemorrhage
Bonnie was 60 when her mother Doris
died at age 81 from colon cancer

I didn't grow up with my mother, but was able to spend time with her during her illness. I was able to forgive her and let go of the past. I understand everything now, and I know that she gave us up so we would have a better life.

\*

SKIP FRANKLIN
Skip was 41 when his mother Dianne
died at age 63 from a series of physical issues

The silver lining for me involved a movie that I watched around the time of my mom's passing, *The Family Man* with Nicholas Cage, Tea Leoni and Don Cheadle. This film gave me a "carpe diem" impetus to get married again and have a family. And today I have two wonderful boys to show for it. I'm so sorry Mom missed my wedding and the birth of my two sons. I know she would have enjoyed that. But that was the silver lining for sure.

\*

KIMBERLY HAWKS
Kimberly was 9 when her father Charles
died at age 32 in a car accident

I've talked about this before. The loss of a human dad at such a young age really drove me to develop my relationship with a divine Father, God. This has enriched my life and ultimately filled a void that could not have been filled in any other way. That has been the silver lining.

\*

VICKI HECKROTH
Vicki was 5 when her mother Bonnie
died at age 27 in an auto accident

I feel I have become a better mother and friend to my surviving daughters. I am more understanding and continually strive for that closeness I have always dreamed about having. I believe my losses have made me a stronger and more compassionate individual. Although sometimes I wish my heart did not break so easily, I am always there with an outstretched hand for those in need.

\*

TERESA HERRING
Teresa was 47 when her father Burton
died at age 65 from brain cancer

For me the silver lining is that I no longer have to wonder if my father will reach out to me, if he misses or loves me. I no longer wait for the Christmas card, the rare meal together. I no longer have to answer questions or give explanations about why he was never around, now he is simply dead. I am no longer waiting for a father's love to rescue me. I am no longer waiting for him to say he is sorry for abandoning me and leaving me with such an unstable home life. I can now move past this part of grieving and into the healing part because he no longer has control of my need for a father.

*

BROOKE NINNI MATTHEWS
Brooke was 38 when her mother JoAnne
died at age 57 from cardiac arrhythmia

My mom and dad separated a few years before her passing, and unfortunately they weren't on good terms, and I then walked away from my dad. I have now reunited with him and gotten closer to him as well as his new wife. I must say it feels pretty good to know I have my dad in my life and my children's lives, after all he's the only parent I have as well as the only grandparent my children have.

*

RUTH PAPALAS
Ruth was 41 when her father David
died at age 62 of a heart attack

The silver lining would have to be that our family doesn't take each other for granted like we used to. We realize that there may not be a "next time" or "next year." We haven't forgotten about Dad. We speak of him often and we smile, laugh and occasionally we cry.

Years ago, our house caught on fire. Dad made several trips back into the flames to make sure that all of us were safe and even threw my one sister out the window when she wouldn't jump. No one was hurt in the fire but we lost almost everything. What survived was an old fashioned bookcase with leaded glass doors that had all of our family pictures in it. When we complained about everything we lost, Mom said "It's just stuff. You can always buy more stuff." Mom and Dad taught us a lot with few words like that.

When Dad was in the hospital, my mom and I were visiting. She was telling him that the AC unit installed in my brother's home, in her opinion, cost too much. Dad said, "Is it in? Does it work? Let it go." When she repeated her concern, Dad repeated, "Is it in? Does it work? Let it go." From that point forward whenever something is bothering Mom or me we still ask, "Is it in? Does it work? Let it go." Then we laugh. I guess it was Dad's way of saying, "Don't sweat the small stuff." Which may be why my definition of hope is what it is.

*

MARY POTTER KENYON
Mary was 26 when her father Byron died at age 61 following a fall
Mary was 51 when her mother Irma died at age 82 from lung cancer

My mother died on my birthday. After a lifetime of struggling to impart a strong faith in her children, I believe my journey to get closer to God began the night of her death, her gift to me. Yes, all she had taught and lived in regards to her own strong faith was the basis for my belief system, but it is as if she watched over me even after her death. My grandson was diagnosed with cancer just a month after her death. I'd get whiffs of cigarette smoke and feathers would appear on my grandson's winter coat during his early treatment. It was after her death that my husband began reading religious books and watching Joyce Meyer on television. He was on his own faith journey and I'm so grateful, because my husband died unexpectedly seventeen months after my mother died.

*

MARY LEE ROBINSON
Mary Lee was 56 when her father Pat
died at age 82 of a massive cerebral hemorrhage

I was always very close to my dad and admired him a lot. Since his death, beginning with his memorial service, it was such a gift to see Dad through the eyes of so many other people. I discovered how many others my dad had touched and how much he was loved. That is a great comfort to me.

\*

JUDY TAYLOR
Judy was 55 when her mum Shirley
died at age 78 from a stroke

Writing and self-expression has been an important part of my life. When my mum died suddenly in February 2011, writing became a wonderful source of support for me to express all my feelings without judgment and get in touch with all my feelings and emotions. Writing helped me find my way through raw grief and helped me discover ways to stay connected with my mum as our new journey began

I shared my writing with friends, family, colleagues and clients and recognized my words touched hearts and helped others also get in touch with their own feelings. As my healing journey unfolded it became obvious that it was important for me to share my journey to help others too. At the end of 2013, my husband and I began researching publishing my journal as a book, and *Mum Moments - Journey Through Grief* was born. Self-publishing my book was an adventure my husband and I embraced together combining our skills and experiences in life. It was an amazing journey where we faced our fears, celebrated our strengths, nurtured our weaknesses and opened our hearts to the world of possibilities. At times everything went our way and at other times we stumbled as we navigated our way through the journey of self-publishing. This project strengthened our relationship and opened our hearts and souls to the importance of living our passion. Launching my book in May 2014, and setting up my Mum Moments - Journey Through Grief Facebook page introduced me to people worldwide who were grieving. Each and every one of them I connected with needed to know they were not alone and it was okay to feel.

It has now become an important part of my life to offer love, comfort and support to people in need. I am now an author, advocate for self-expression, and supporter of human beings in need. This is definitely my silver lining.

*

## HEATHER WALLACE-REY
Heather was 40 when her father John
died suddenly at age 71 of a massive heart attack

There were moments during the grieving process when I did not believe there could EVER be any kind of a silver lining in grief. As time has progressed however, I have come to recognize a number of different silver linings as a part of this process. One silver lining in this process is that I am slowly (sometimes too slowly, I think) learning to give myself grace. Before the death of my father, I was a complete and utter perfectionist, especially with my expectations of myself. Through the grieving process, these impossible expectations of myself, which had heightened due to grief, often made me impatient and ridiculously frustrated with why I seemed unable to "heal" faster while those around me seemed to be able to move on much more quickly. I realize now that this may not have been completely true, I may just have seen only what they wanted me to see.

What I have learned and am continuing to learn is that while it is completely possible to continue ongoing, burdensome, impossibly high expectations for yourself, the misery these expectations create in a person's life is both terrible and also incomprehensible. Albeit a little too slow for my own liking, I am learning that giving myself grace is a much better place to be. I am now giving myself the grace to feel whatever I need to feel, the grace to not feel that I have to be perfect, and the grace to allow myself to not have to feel immediately healed.

As I navigate my way through that grace, my faith has taken some turns for the better. It has allowed people to speak into my life through their own experiences with grief. I was able to admit to others that I am far from perfect. I was also able to admit to myself that I don't have to be perfect or strong enough to carry my burden alone.

Another silver lining that has resulted from my loss is my ability to minister to others who are dealing with loss. Before the loss of my father, I often went to funerals and memorial services but never knew what to say. I was terrified of saying the wrong thing, and absolutely did not know how to follow up with those who were grieving. I have been fortunate enough to meet people who are good at dealing with grief, not only because of their own experiences, but because they have such a heart for compassion and know how to be there for others through the grief process. I would not have necessarily put myself in that category before three and a half years ago.

I work for a church, and have for almost my whole adult life. As such, I understand and am good at expressing compassion but I was still terrified that I might say the wrong thing to someone who was suffering. I learned early on that my worries were generally unfounded. In my own experience, I just wanted people who tried to understand my pain, who offered to be there for me and who understood that they did not need to have the perfect words. Or any words at all. There are no perfect words. In many cases, they just needed to answer their phones and listen to me. They just needed to show up. They just needed to be present in my life. I also have a special place in my heart for all those who have remembered me in a compassionate way during those first holidays without my dad, and on the first anniversary of his death.

My silver lining has come in the way of an answer to a questioning prayer: how can I help someone else who is going through this? Today I am much better equipped to sit quietly with someone who is grieving and to attend memorial services and funerals without feeling awkward because I know - to someone who is trying to survive grief - it's not about ME. It's about THEM. It's about putting myself and my feelings completely aside and quietly holding the hand of someone who needs me.

My third silver lining has been a program sponsored by the Presbyterian Church (PCUSA) that is appearing in communities throughout the United States called "Faith and Grief." There are many Presbyterian churches that are now putting on these "Faith and Grief Luncheons" once a month, which allow people from all faiths to come together in community and share stories of grief, to pray together, read scripture and eat lunch together. But, most of all, it brings people together to sit with others who are at different parts of the grief process as a reminder that none of us are alone, and that we can traverse grief together.

*

If you happen to think of me, remember how I used to be.
And when, while you're pausing after I am laid to rest,
Take a moment to recall that of me that was best.
RALPH LONG

*

CHAPTER EIGHTEEN

# OUR HOPE

*Be like the birds, sing after every storm.*
BETH MENDE CONNY

Hope is the fuel that propels us forward, urges us to get out of bed each morning. It is the promise that tomorrow will be better than today. Each breath we take and each footprint we leave is a measure of hope. So is hope possible in the aftermath of loss? If so, where do we find it?

*

SOPHIE BLOWERS
Sophie was 50 when her mother Amy
died at age 79 of internal bleeding

Hope is not giving up or giving in. Believing that there is some reason to take another breath. My family is always a source of hope. Hope is my grandchildren, my job, my faith, and often it is my dog. Hope is whatever brings you peace at the moment you need it. Hope is whatever keeps you from giving up.

\*

CHRISTINE DUMINIAK
Christine was 57 when her mother Ann
died at age 86 from an abdominal aortic aneurysm

Hope is a gift from God that helps us look forward to better times. It is like a shining light beaming through the darkness that we can reach out to.

\*

BONNIE FORSHEY
Bonnie was an infant when her father Andrew
died at age 41 from a cerebral hemorrhage
Bonnie was 60 when her mother Doris
died at age 81 from colon cancer

I hope that I will leave this earth knowing that I was a good mother and grandmother. I want to leave good memories behind. We all do things we are not proud of, take the time to apologize, you may not have another chance.

\*

SKIP FRANKLIN
Skip was 41 when his mother Dianne
died at age 63 from a series of physical issues

"Faith is the substance of things hoped for, the evidence of things not seen," is one of my favorite quotes. This, coupled with an "all things work together for good" conviction, comprises my definition of hope. How can a difficult event result in good? I witness it every day. In this case, it's about people sharing their stories, giving, loving and embracing others going through similar circumstances. My hope increases as these ripples expand and reach to the far side of the lake to bless even more. And then those, in turn, help and bless others.

*

KIMBERLY HAWKS
Kimberly was 9 when her father Charles
died at age 32 in a car accident

I think "hope" involves the knowledge that what loss and hardship one has gone through will ultimately help and bless others. It is the hope that all things can "work together for good." Even traumatic life-changing events can lead to positive impact. And for me, my music and ministry are evidence of that hope. And seeing the blessings increase because of it.

*

VICKI HECKROTH
Vicki was 5 when her mother Bonnie
died at age 27 in an auto accident

Hope to me is being able to make my mother proud of me and the person I have become. To know that there will come a day when I can once again be with her, and that this time it will be forever. Knowing that no matter how low I am made to feel on this earth, that she will always love and care for me.

*

TERESA HERRING
Teresa was 47 when her father Burton
died at age 65 from brain cancer

For me hope is the ability to look at the future and see something different, something wonderful. It is the ability to come from such an ugly place, a place of unimaginable pain, a place many wouldn't survive and learn from all the ugly bad pain and still look to the future with wonder. Hope for me is the belief that no matter where you came from, where you are right now, where you may be tomorrow, things will get better. Even if all you see is ugly around you, it will get better. It is taking a step. Even if you don't know where you are going, you are at least taking a step.

*

BROOKE NINNI MATTHEWS
Brooke was 38 when her mother JoAnne
died at age 57 from cardiac arrhythmia

Learn to forgive, you may not forget and nor do you have to, but forgive yourself and those who may have hurt you, or done you wrong. Live your life to the fullest with love in your heart.

*

RUTH PAPALAS
Ruth was 41 when her father David
died at age 62 of a heart attack

At first this was the most difficult question to answer. After considering it, the best answer I can give is a Bob Marley quote that has been my ringtone on my cellphone for over ten years, "Every Little Thing Gonna Be All Right."

*

MARY LEE ROBINSON
Mary Lee was 56 when her father Pat
died at age 82 of a massive cerebral hemorrhage

Because of my dad's example, I suppose my biggest hope is that I can touch lives and leave the world a better place, as he did. Dad volunteered quite a few places, but chief among them was fifty years of service to the Boy Scouts of America. Some of my high school friends still tell me stories of admiration about him. Dad's big cause was Boy Scouts of America. I would like to make just such an impression, a smaller one, on improving the treatment of grievers. If I accomplish nothing else, I hope that I can do that. Dad would approve.

\*

JUDY TAYLOR
Judy was 55 when her mum Shirley
died at age 78 from a stroke

My desire is for both myself and others to experience peace and love as we all journey through life. My hope is for us all to connect with the pure essence of love that radiates from our hearts and to support others when they need it and be supported when we need it. Life has many twists and turns so I would like to be able to accept whatever presents and choose to respond to life for the benefit of my highest good and the highest good of others. I hope to both give and receive love, comfort, support and compassion on my journey.

\*

HEATHER WALLACE-REY
Heather was 40 when her father John
died suddenly at age 71 of a massive heart attack

In Jeremiah 29:11, the Bible says, "For I know the plans I have for you," declares the Lord, "plans to prosper you and not to harm you, plans to give you hope and a future." In the years leading up to my father's death, this was always my "go to" verse. It has taken me three and a half years to restore some measure of the hope that I used to have, or to be able to read this verse through the same eyes as before. For a long time, the definitions of hope and promise in my life felt very much like they had been stolen, ripped right out from under my feet. I have always believed that hope is an expectation or desire that something is supposed to happen. Before losing my dad, perhaps I had some vision of hope that was a little naïve, as I believed that hope was this entity that was not only an expectation that something is supposed to happen, but fulfillment of those expectations would be beautiful, wonderful and lovely. I never expected that disappointed expectations and desires or loss could rob you of that hope, or change that hope into something ugly or unrecognizable.

After my initial loss, my hope and faith regressed to that of a seven-year-old child. The only thing I really hoped for was some sort of miracle that would bring my dad back to me. I had many, many, many moments where I believed that both my hope and my faith had been stolen by grief. During this process, I did lots of reading, not devotional books on grief, but largely true stories of those with immense grief and loss and how these survivors have continually not only coped but also gone on with their lives. One book that helped me in completely inexplicable ways is *Night*, by holocaust survivor Elie Wiesel. The horrors and loss that he dealt with as a small child in a concentration camp, and the fact that he is still able to talk about hope and faith has not only been an inspiration, but also such a comfort to me. One of Wiesel's quotes is, "Just as despair can come to one only from other human beings, hope, too, can be given to one only by other human beings." In some of the most difficult moments of my grief, I read and reread this quote over and over.

For what seemed like an excruciatingly long time, I believed that hope was an object: something similar to a material possession that could actually be stolen from you. In personifying my grief and trying to cope with it, I felt that my hope was lost or stolen. I realized as part of this process that hope and faith are not objects. They can't be stolen or lost, like a suitcase or an umbrella. Unfortunately in the darkest of times, it can be hard to dig deep and find that hope and that faith. However, they are still there. The knowledge that my hope and faith were still very much with me began to come back the moment I realized that not only had they been present the whole time, but the person I was before the death of my dad and the person I am still becoming are not completely different people, but are also not the same.

Grief has changed my life, the way I view the world, and the person that I will be from this day forward. I still have hope. I still have hope that there is good in the world. Much of my hope HAS been restored by the goodness of the people surrounding me who have loved me, reached out to me, and not let me drown during the worst parts of this process. However, my hope today is different from what it was prior to my father's death. It is a hope that comes with the knowledge that there are hopes that will be dashed, and prayers that will not be answered in the way you want them to be answered.

For a while, I thought my hope was gone. I thought all hope was lost. What I realized is that hope is still very much a part of me, but life still does not always turn out the way you plan. You can have hope and grief. They can coexist. As this process continues, I can only pray that my hope gets stronger and more positively charged, while the grief continues to lessen.

*

One smile can change a day.
One hug can change a life.
One hope can change a destiny.
LYNDA CHELDELIN FELL

\*

CHAPTER NINETEEN

# OUR JOURNEY

*Be soft. Do not let the world make you hard. Do not let the pain*
*make you hate. Do not let bitterness steal your sweetness.*
KURT VONNEGUT

Every journey through loss is as unique as one's fingerprint, for we experience different beliefs, different desires, different needs, different tolerances, and often we walk different roads. Though we may not see anyone else on the path, we are never truly alone for more walk behind, beside, and in front of us. In this chapter lies the writers' answers to the final question posed: What would you like the world to know about your grief journey?

\*

SOPHIE BLOWERS
Sophie was 50 when her mother Amy
died at age 79 of internal bleeding

It sucked. It was awful. But if I had to do it again, I would change very little. If one is presented with a horrible situation, find some purpose in it. Don't let pain be in vain. Tell your story, help someone, volunteer...do something. Use your experience to help someone else. I know some people are offended by the saying, "Everything happens for a reason." I have to believe that there is a purpose, or at the least I will be able to use this experience for the greater good. I must believe that for my own sanity. I will keep moving forward, if for no other reason than to find that reason and purpose. Perhaps I will be the shoulder that someone needs. I will understand and have empathy because I have been there, done that and reach the person no one else could reach. Will this make the loss worthwhile? Absolutely not. Will it make the grief a little more bearable? For me, on my path, it will.

\*

CHRISTINE DUMINIAK
Christine was 57 when her mother Ann
died at age 86 from an abdominal aortic aneurysm

I have found that the pain from grief can definitely lessen over time, especially if we find ways to reach out to family and friends and others to help fill the void.

\*

BONNIE FORSHEY
Bonnie was an infant when her father Andrew
died at age 41 from a cerebral hemorrhage
Bonnie was 60 when her mother Doris
died at age 81 from colon cancer

I used to harbor so much resentment because I was abandoned as a child. I didn't know all of the facts, so I missed out on really getting to know my mother. During the time that she was ill, I learned all of the facts and was able to let go of the anger. We became very close. I wish I hadn't been so stubborn, I missed out on so much. I think of her every day.

\*

SKIP FRANKLIN
Skip was 41 when his mother Dianne
died at age 63 from a series of physical issues

I think this journey has led me to a wonderful community, a village so to speak. And the inspiration I get from them is incredible. I think it's important to remember that we are not the only ones going through an experience, and that we can learn so much from others. While every journey is unique and individual, we don't have to take that journey alone. There are some amazing hearts out there willing to take that journey with us. Part of our journey is to find them!

\*

KIMBERLY HAWKS
Kimberly was 9 when her father Charles
died at age 32 in a car accident

I want people to know that the grief journey may never end completely. But if you can use it to help others and bless others, that it can be very fulfilling and enriching and can become an amazing journey. I think this book is evidence of exactly that.

\*

VICKI HECKROTH
Vicki was 5 when her mother Bonnie
died at age 27 in an auto accident

I want others to think about what they are saying to a young child concerning death. Do not tell a five-year-old that their loved one is just sleeping. It may seem like a good idea at the time but from someone who has been there, it is not a good idea at all. I also want others to understand that when a parent with young children dies, those young children need their world to remain constant. Never tell a child she is fat, ugly or reminds you too much of their deceased parent. Words can hurt more than you can imagine and once self-esteem is destroyed, it is hard to get back. Death is very different than divorce in that you do not have to be in competition with the person. And never ever try to force feelings upon a child such as making them call another person "mom" or "dad." That should be each child's choice and many times, when forced, it makes the child feel guilty like they abandoned the parent they lost.

*

TERESA HERRING
Teresa was 47 when her father Burton
died at age 65 from brain cancer

I was and have been so angry at my father that I felt no need to grieve for his death. I was very wrong and, even though he was a very little part of my life, I need to work through the stages of grief. Grief is work and it is hard, but you are never alone in grief. When I stop long enough to listen to myself I am sure that my father was in some ways good, and to some people he was wonderful. I had a different experience with him in my life. Yes, it is sad, but I am learning to move past the anger and let myself grieve my loss. We have to learn to be as gentle with ourselves as we are to others. There is no time limit on the process and it could take years as it has with me, but it is possible to move on and be happy.

*

BROOKE NINNI MATTHEWS
Brooke was 38 when her mother JoAnne
died at age 57 from cardiac arrhythmia

I was born with a heart condition and was unable to drive, so my mom took me everywhere I needed to go or wanted to go. I never realized how much I depended on my mom, until she was no longer around. I'm forty-two-years-old and I still need my mom. I guess it doesn't matter how old you are, you will always need your mom. My mom taught me many things in life, except how to get through life without her.

194

\*

RUTH PAPALAS
Ruth was 41 when her father David
died at age 62 of a heart attack

My dad has been gone for over fifteen years. I don't cry over him being gone now, but I do think about Dad every day. How would things be different if he was still alive? What would Dad think about this? Dad would have really liked that. Dad would be really sad about this. That sort of thing.

His photos are around my house and I see them every day. I look at them and remember and smile because there's a story, a memory with each picture. Certain subjects in conversations make me think of Dad and what his reactions would be. If someone brings up fishing, or Canada or a good school teacher – I think of him. Sometimes my memories take me back to the island where we used to set up the tent, or "the one that got away" with my favorite fishing plug. There are times when we are simply buying a loaf of bread and I think of Dad. I always feel the weight of the bread. If it's heavy, I think Dad would have liked this one.

It's the special moments though that I think of Dad and the events that he's not here for. I mentioned it in an earlier question, but that's the worst time for me. Watching my son and daughter graduate and later marry without my dad there, or watching my brother give away both of my sisters at their weddings because my dad wasn't there. Seeing Dad's picture on memorial tables at graduations or weddings hurts my heart that he's not there. Holding my first grandson for the first time took me back to when I had my preemie daughter and Dad rushed to the hospital to see us. Realizing that he will never get to take his great-grandson fishing or that my grandson will never know my dad makes me sad.

I didn't just lose my dad at one point in time – I lost him in every aspect of my life for the rest of my life and I miss him. I always will.

\*

MARY LEE ROBINSON
Mary Lee was 56 when her father Pat
died at age 82 of a massive cerebral hemorrhage

Anyone who knew my dad and anyone who attended his final ceremony would tell you that his was a life well lived. That is Dad's main lesson to me: to live your life in a way that matters. Seeing how loved Dad was by others gave me a lot of comfort. Knowing that he had a positive influence on so many other people is comforting too. Between that and how easy he made it to plan things for him left me in a very good place in the aftermath of a very big loss. I will always miss Dad, but that is soothed by all of the light and positivity around him. He was a good man, it was a good life, he made a good exit. Love you, Dad!

\*

JUDY TAYLOR
Judy was 55 when her mum Shirley
died at age 78 from a stroke

Through my darkest moments on my grief journey I have also discovered the shining light that is always waiting to guide me each step of the way. In terms of love, my mum touched my heart when she gave birth to me. She touched my heart when she died. She continues to touch my heart in the afterlife. We are connected forever.

\*

HEATHER WALLACE-REY
Heather was 40 when her father John
died suddenly at age 71 of a massive heart attack

I think most people who have known me forever, those who have known me only a short time, and those who continue to meet me would tell you I do not strike any of them as a completely off-my-rocker, grief-stricken banshee. Most people would describe me as a normal person. Okay, maybe not my children, but that has less to do with grief, and more to do with the fact that every child needs at least one crazy parent with which to credit the future therapy they will need.

I would like people who are going through the grieving process to know that it has taken me three and a half years, lots of love and care from those around me, lots of leaning on those who have been through this or are currently going through it, professional counseling, professional medical help and antidepressants, a monthly support group, and being able to write my own book, *Faith, Grief and Pass the Chocolate Pudding*, due out March 2016, to be able to get through the craziness I have experienced through this process.

For those who have experienced recent loss, what I would really like to share with all of you is this: you can believe yourself to be the strongest, most faithful, most independent, self-sufficient person in the free world and you might still need help in figuring out how to keep grief at bay. It doesn't mean you are not strong enough or that you have lost either your mind or your ability to function as a normal person. It means you are human. Please don't allow pride or fear of what others might think keep you from getting the help you need to get you through grief: no matter what form of help you need.

My biggest regret throughout this process was that I waited so long to seek help from others because I was so afraid to admit that, whether or not I had a smile on my face for all the world to see, grief was shredding me apart from the inside out. I wish I had decided to seek professional help within the first two months. I wish I had decided to look for support groups within the first month after my father died. I could have saved myself about two years of identity crisis, useless struggle, loneliness and convincing myself that nobody else on this whole planet was as crazy as I was, simply by finding other people who had experienced a similar loss sooner in my grieving process.

Everyone's loss is different, but that doesn't mean that other people haven't been where you are and aren't willing to share their stories with you. What I wish I had known much sooner, and I want everyone facing loss of a parent to know, is that I cannot get my father back. Although he lives on in my memories and in the hearts of all who knew and loved him, I can't get him back. But I CAN get myself back; maybe even a more compassionate, more peaceful, more full-of-grace version of myself. And so can you.

There are people who will tell you that it gets easier. I do not believe that it gets easier, but it does get less awful. There will be good days and bad days, easy days and difficult days, emotionally charged days and peaceful days but -as time passes - it DOES get less awful. If today is not the "less awful" day for you - please hang on, because I promise there will be less awful days ahead.

\*

CHAPTER TWENTY

# FINDING THE SUNRISE

One night in my own journey, I had one of *those* dreams: a vivid nightmare that stays with you. I was running westward in a frantic attempt to catch the setting sun as it descended below the horizon. Rapidly advancing from behind was nightfall; foreboding and frightening, it was a pitch black abyss. And it was coming directly for me. I ran desperately, as fast as my legs could go, toward the sunset, but my attempt was futile; it descended below the horizon, out of my reach. Oh, the looming nightfall was terrifying! But it was clear that if I wanted to ever see the sun again, I had to stop running west and, instead, turn around and walk east to begin my journey through the great murky abyss, the nightfall of grief. For just as there would be no rainbow without the rain, the sun only rises on the other side of night.

The message was clear: it was futile to avoid my grief; I had to allow it to swallow me whole. Then, and only then, would I find my way through it and out the other side.

I remember reading in a bereavement book that if we don't allow ourselves to experience the full scope of the journey, it will come back to bite us. I couldn't fathom how it could get any worse, but I knew I didn't want to test that theory. So I gave in and allowed my grief to swallow me whole. I allowed myself to wail on my daughter's bedroom floor. I penned my deep emotions, regardless of who might read it. I created a national radio show to openly and candidly discuss our journeys with anyone who wanted to call in. And I allowed myself to sink to the bottom of the fiery pits of hell. This, in turn, lit a fire under me, so to speak, to find a way out.

Today, I'm often asked how I manage my grief so well. Some assume that because I have found peace and joy, I'm simply avoiding my grief. Others believe that because I work in the bereavement field, I'm wallowing in self-pity. Well, which is it?

Neither. I will miss my child with every breath I take. Just like you, I will always have my moments: the painful holidays, birthdays, death anniversaries, a song or smell that evokes an unexpected memory. But I have also found purpose, beauty and joy again. It takes hard work and determination to overcome profound grief, and it also takes the ability to let go and succumb to the journey. Do not be afraid of the tears, sorrow, and heartbreak; they are a natural reaction, and are imperative to your healing.

As you walk your own path, avail yourself to whatever bereavement tools that might ease your discomfort, for each one was created by someone who walked in your shoes and understands the heartache. While there are many wonderful bereavement resources available, what brings comfort to one person might irritate the next. Bereavement tools are not one-size-fits-all, so if one tool doesn't work, find another.

Lastly, grief is not something we get "over," like a mountain. Rather, it is something we get "through," like the rapids of Niagara Falls. Without the kayak and paddle. And plenty of falls. But it's also survivable. And if others had survived this wretched journey, why not me? And why not you?

On the following pages are the baby steps I took to put hell in my rearview mirror. They took great effort at first, and lots of patience. Like any dedicated routine, it got easier over time, and the reward of finding balance in my life was worth every step.

## 1. VALIDATING OUR EMOTIONS

The first step is to validate your emotions. When we talk about our deep heartbreak, we aren't ruminating in our sorrow or feeling sorry for ourselves. By discussing it, we are actually processing it. If we aren't allowed to process it, then it becomes silent grief. Silent grief is deadly grief.

Find a friend who will patiently listen while you discuss your loss for fifteen minutes every day. Set the timer, and ask them not to say anything during those fifteen minutes. Explain that it is important for you to just ramble without interruption, guidance, or judgment. You need not have the same listener each time, but practice this step <u>every</u> day.

## 2. COMPASSIONATE THOUGHTS

Find yourself a quiet spot. It can be your favorite chair, in your car, in your office, or even in your garden. Then clear your head and for five minutes think nothing but compassionate thoughts about yourself. Not your spouse, not your children, not your coworkers, but yourself.

Having trouble? Fill in the blanks below, and then give yourself permission to *really* validate those positive qualities. Do this every day.


I have a _____

Example: good heart, gentle soul, witty personality

I make a _____

Example: good lasagna, potato salad, scrapbook, quilt

I'm a good_____

Example: friend, gardener, knitter, painter, poem writer

People would say I'm _____

Example: funny, kind, smart, gentle, generous, humble, creative

## 3. TENDER LOVING CARE

While grieving, it is important to consider yourself in the intensive care unit of Grief United Hospital, and treat accordingly. How would nurses treat you if you were their patient in the ICU? They would be compassionate, gentle, and allow for plenty of rest. That is exactly how you should treat yourself. Also, consider soothing your physical self with TLC as an attentive way to honor your emotional pain. This doesn't mean you have to book an expensive massage. If wearing fuzzy blue socks offers a smidgen of comfort, then wear them unabashedly. If whipped cream on your cocoa offers a morsel of pleasure, then indulge unapologetically.

Treating our five senses to anything that offers a perception of delight might not erase the emotional heartache, but it will offer a reminder that not all pleasure is lost. List five ways you can offer yourself tender loving care, and then incorporate at least three into your day, every day. With practice, the awareness of delight eventually becomes effortless, and is an important step toward regaining joy.

TLC suggestions:
- Shower or bathe with a lovely scented soap
- Soak in a warm tub with Epsom salts or a splash of bath oil
- Wear a pair of extra soft socks
- Light a fragrant candle
- Listen to relaxing music
- Apply a rich lotion to your skin before bed
- Indulge in a few bites of your favorite treat
- Enjoy a mug of your favorite soothing herbal tea
- Add whipped cream to a steaming mug of cocoa
- Take a short road trip along a scenic route
- Take a nap
- Treat yourself to a homemade facial
- Stay in your pajamas all day

## 4. SEE THE BEAUTY

Listening to the birds outside my bedroom window every morning was something I had loved since childhood. But when Aly died, I found myself deaf and blind to the beauty around me. My world had become colorless and silent. On one particular morning as I struggled to get out of bed, I halfheartedly noticed the birds chirping outside my bedroom window. My heart sank as I realized that they had been chirping all along, but I was now deaf to their morning melody. Panic set in as I concluded that I would never enjoy life's beauty ever again. Briefly entertaining suicide to escape the profound pain, I quickly ruled it out. My family had been through so much already, I couldn't dump further pain on them. But in order to survive the heartbreak, I had to find a way to allow beauty back into my life.

So on that particular morning as I lay in bed, I forced myself to listen and really *hear* the birds. Every morning from that point forward, I repeated that same exercise. With persistent practice, it became easier and then eventually effortless to appreciate the birds' chirping and singsongs. Glorious beauty and sounds have once again returned to my world.

Profound grief can appear to rob our world of all beauty. Yet the truth is, and despite our suffering, beauty continues to surround us. The birds continue to sing, flowers continue to bloom, the surf continues to ebb and flow. Reconnecting to our surroundings helps us to reintegrate back into our environment.

Begin by acknowledging one small pleasantry each day. Perhaps your ears register the sound of singing birds. Or you catch the faint scent of warm cookies as you walk past a bakery. Or notice the sun's illumination of a nearby red rosebush. Give yourself permission to notice one pleasantry, and allow it to *really* register.

Here are some suggestions:

- Listen to the birds sing (hearing)
- Observe pretty cloud formations (sight)
- Visit a nearby park and listen to the children (hearing)
- Notice the pretty colors of blooming flowers (sight)
- Light a fragrant candle (scent)
- See the beauty in the sunset (sight)
- Attend a local recital, concert, play, or comedy act (hearing)
- Wear luxury socks (touch)
- Wrap yourself in a soft scarf or sweater (touch)
- Indulge in whipped cream on your cocoa (taste)
- Enjoy a Hershey's chocolate kiss (taste)

## 5. PROTECT YOUR HEALTH

After our daughter's accident I soon found myself fighting an assortment of viruses including head colds, stomach flus, sore throats and more, compounding my already frazzled emotions. Studies show that profound grief throws our body into "flight or fight" syndrome for months and months, which is very hard on our physical body. Thus, it becomes critical to guard our physical health. Incorporating a few changes into our daily routine feels hard at first, but soon gets easy. Plus, a stronger physical health helps to strengthen our coping skills.

Below are a few suggestions to consider adding to your daily routine to help your physical self withstand the emotional upheaval.

- Practice good sleep hygiene
- Drink plenty of water
- Take a short walk outside every day
- Resist simple carbohydrates (I'm a food addict, so I know that avoiding simple carbs is worth its weight in gold)
- Add antioxidant-rich food
- Keep a light calendar and guard your time carefully, don't allow others to dictate and overflow your schedule

## 6. FIND AN OUTLET

For a long time in the grief journey, everything is painful. In the early days, just getting out of bed and taking a shower can be exhausting. Housecleaning, grocery shopping, and routine errands often take a backseat or disappear altogether. As painful as it is, it's very important to find an outlet that gets you out of bed each day. Finding something to distract you from the pain, occupy your mind, and soothe your senses can be tricky, but possible. Performing a repetitive action can calm your mood, and even result in a new craft or gifts to give. Beginning a new outlet may feel exhausting at first, just remember that the first step is always the hardest. And you don't have to do it forever, just focus on it for the time being.

Possible activities include:

- Learn to mold chocolate or make soap
- Learn how to bead, knit, crochet, or quilt
- Volunteer at a local shelter
- Learn a new sport such as golf or kayaking
- Create a memorial garden in a forgotten part of the yard
- Join Pinterest
- Doodle or draw
- Mold clay
- Learn to scrapbook
- Join a book club

Grief is hell on earth. It truly is. But when walking through hell, your only option is to keep going. Eventually the hell ends, the dark night fades to dawn, and the sun begins its ascent once again.

Just keep going and you, too, will find the sunrise.

*Lynda Cheldelin Fell*

*Hope is like the sun, which, as we journey toward it,
casts the shadow of our burden behind us.*
SAMUEL SMILES

*

# ABOUT US

\*

SOPHIE BLOWERS
Sophie was 50 when her mother Amy
died at age 79 of internal bleeding
SophieBlowers1@gmail.com

Stephanie Blowers was born in North Virginia in the mid 1960s. She was a stay-at-home mom, raising and home educating her four children for twenty-five years. Once her youngest graduated from high school, Stephanie returned to school herself and earned a degree in paralegal studies. Stephanie now works for a pro bono law firm. Stephanie's true passion is in the support of the newly bereaved, using her heightened empathy skills to create a safe place for the griever as the overwhelming reality of loss is realized.

\*

### CHRISTINE DUMINIAK
Christine was 57 when her mother Ann
died at age 86 from an abdominal aortic aneurysm
www.ChristineDuminiak.com    \*    ChrisDuminiak@aol.com

Christine Duminiak is a Certified Grief Recovery Specialist, radio host, author, speaker, and founder of Prayer Wave for After-Death Communications.

Duminiak has been a guest on many TV and radio shows, including Fox & Friends, Good Day Philadelphia, The God Squad, the Arizona Midday Show, NBC, CBS, and Coast-to-Coast AM and is a frequent keynote speaker at grief seminars.

Christine is the author of *Heaven Talks to Children, God's Gift of Love: After-Death Communications*, and the new children's book, *Grammy Visits From Heaven*.

\*
WENDY EVANS
Wendy was 14 when her father Dwight
died at age 32 in a plane crash
wendyconley1976@gmail.com

Wendy Evans was born in Middletown, Ohio, in the late 1950s. She now lives in Kennesaw, Georgia, and has worked in the staffing industry for twenty-seven years.

Happily married to her husband Robb, they share four children, one grandchild, and their two dogs Simon and Garfunkel.

*

BONNIE FORSHEY
Bonnie was an infant when her father Andrew
died at age 41 from a cerebral hemorrhage
Bonnie was 60 when her mother Doris
died at age 81 from colon cancer
bonnieforshey@msn.com

Bonnie Forshey was born in Lewistown, Pennsylvania, and raised in New Castle, Delaware. She later moved to Swainsboro, Georgia, and attended Emanuel County Junior College where she earned the Science Merit Award and graduated with her A.S. degree. Bonnie then attended Gordon State College in Barnesville, Georgia, earning a B.S. in Nursing. She spent most of her life working in medical-surgical, geriatrics, rehabilitation and long-term care facilities. Bonnie raised two children and worked as a nursing assistant, unit secretary, and in medical records while putting herself through school. Bonnie currently resides in both Port Royal, Pennsylvania, and Brandon, Florida, and has two grandsons.

\*

SKIP FRANKLIN
Skip was 41 when his mother Dianne
died at age 63 from a series of physical issues

 Selim "Skip" Franklin is a serial entrepreneur who has founded over a dozen companies to date. Skip co-founded Amaze Inc! in 1990, which teamed with cartoonist Gary Larson to launch The Far Side Computer Calendar, earning Product of the Year honors. In 1995, Skip also co-founded an online adventure magazine called MountainZone.com that covered several famous Mount Everest expeditions and as well as other mountain events around the globe.

After moving from Seattle to Nashville, Skip has been involved with musical artists and festivals. He has successfully sold six companies in his career and is in the process of starting more. He is also developing a resource and mentorship association to help entrepreneurs worldwide called Serial Entrepreneurs Anonymous. Skip is working on his first book that includes his whacky Far Side tales, due out in 2016.

\*
DONNA GORE
Donna was 26 when her father Donald
died by homicide in 1980
www.donnagore.com

Donna Gore earned a Master's degree in speech and language pathology and became immersed in all things medical from both sides of the bed as a direct care rehabilitation therapist.

Born with spastic cerebral palsy, she has endured fifty-eight surgeries in her lifetime. She is a highly regarded accomplished advocate for all types of crime victims-survivors, persons with disabilities, and LGBT.

For the past fifteen years, Donna has worked as a human services advocate for the State of Connecticut, serving blind and visually impaired clients. Donna also hosts Shattered Lives, a weekly radio show, and loves to write about different aspects of homicidal violence.

*

### KIMBERLY HAWKS
Kimberly was 9 when her father Charles
died at age 32 in a car accident
kimberlyhawksmusic@gmail.com

Kimberly Hawks has been entertaining people her entire life. She was born in Lansing, Michigan, and spent her young childhood playing in the woods with her three younger siblings. After the death of her father when Kimberly was nine, her family moved to New Mexico. There she began to sing at local rodeos and sporting events. Kimberly was the first female vocalist to make it into the New Mexico All State Choir from her high school. She later attended New Mexico State University as a Vocal Performance Major.

In 2004, Kimberly joined the United States Air Force. She is an adventurous person and desired to serve her country. Two weeks into active duty, music found her yet again. Kimberly was asked to audition for one of the Air Force bands and later toured the world as part of the prestigious Tops In Blue entertainment unit.

Kimberly also saw a lot of death and experienced traumatic challenges. Her quest is to help others facing similar challenges, and she continues to use her music as part of this healing mission.

Today Kimberly is a singer-songwriter, author and speaker headquartered in Nashville, Tennessee, where she is working on her upcoming CD and book.

*

VICKI HECKROTH
Vicki was 5 when her mother Bonnie
died at age 27 in an auto accident

Vicki Heckroth was born in Spencer, Iowa, the second child of Bonnie and Gail Handy. She was welcomed at home by her older sister Terrie, and her brother Rodney was born three years later. Vicki spent her early years in Worthington, Minnesota, before moving to Greenville, Iowa, at age ten. Vicki was raised by her father and stepmother Shirley. She also had two half-siblings, Kristi and Brian. Vicki has been through a lot in life beginning from the tender age of five when her mom died in an automobile accident. She has weathered two very abusive relationships, having a granddaughter born with some issues, and losing her youngest child and only son, 17-year-old Matthew, in 2000 to suicide.

Vicki is disabled from rheumatoid arthritis and several other health issues, though she was healthy until her son passed away. She has been married for twenty-five years, and has two daughters, thirty-five year-old Heidi and thirty-three year-old Melissa. She resides in Iowa, where she breeds Chihuahuas.

\*

TERESA HERRING
Teresa was 47 when her father Burton
died at age 65 from brain cancer
Teresaherring@gmail.com

Teresa spent her early years in Nashville, Tennessee, and now lives in Panama City Beach, Florida. She has one older sister and no brothers.

Teresa is the mother of two sons. Her oldest son, Matt has two daughters (Kendra and Hayden), and her youngest son Brandon has two daughters and one son (Allison, Madison and Logan). Teresa graduated from college and has worked her entire career in the medical billing field. Teresa enjoys spending time with family, traveling, the beach, snorkeling and scuba diving.

\*

## BROOKE NINNI MATTHEWS
Brooke was 38 when her mother JoAnne
died at age 57 from cardiac arrhythmia

Brooke Ninni Matthews was born in Pennsylvania and raised in the small town of Oley Valley. She was born with a congenital heart defect and had her first heart surgery when she was just two days old. Brooke could not do things like sports, play out in the snow, etc, but her parents made sure she had a good life. She left high school at the age of sixteen, and started working in a sewing factory with her mother.

Brooke married at age eighteen and divorced a year later. She then met her second husband and at the age of twenty-four she fostered a little boy, who is now her eighteen-year-old adopted son. Five years later she fostered a little girl who is now her twelve-year-old adopted daughter. Brooke and her husband celebrated twenty years of marriage in November 2015.

\*
RUTH PAPALAS
Ruth was 41 when her father David
died at age 62 of a heart attack

Ruth Papalas was born and raised in Northeast Ohio, and earned an Business Administration degree in 1999. Her career includes several restaurants and housing authorities in the Ohio region. Ruth recently relocated and now resides with her retired husband in South Carolina, where her son and daughter-in-law also reside. Ruth also has a daughter and son-in-law who live in Ohio.

She loves to spend time with her family, friends and dogs. She enjoys going to garage sales and locating unique items. She loves to travel, especially to Jamaica. Since relocating to South Carolina, Ruth met new friends including author Mary Lee Robinson, whom Ruth assisted in the writing of *The Widow or Widower Next Door*.

217

\*

MARY POTTER KENYON

Mary was 26 when her father Byron died at age 61 following a fall
Mary was 51 when her mother Irma died at age 82 from lung cancer
www.marypotterkenyon.com    \*    marypotterkenyon@gmail.com

Mary Potter Kenyon graduated from the University of Northern Iowa and is a reporter for the Manchester Press newspaper in Iowa. She is a widely published author, workshop presenter and sought after public speaker.

Familius has published four of her books: *Coupon Crazy: The Science, the Savings and the Stories Behind America's Extreme Obsession*, *Chemo-Therapist: How Cancer Cured a Marriage*, *Refined By Fire: A Journey of Grief and Grace*, and is co-author of *Mary & Me: A Lasting Link Through Ink*. Several of Mary's devotions were published in Zondervan's *Hope in the Mourning* Bible and an essay about the connection between grief and creativity was published in the January/February issue of *Poets & Writers* magazine. Mary lives in Iowa with two of her eight children.

\*

MARY LEE ROBINSON
Mary Lee was 56 when her father Pat
died at age 82 of a massive cerebral hemorrhage
thewidoworwidowernextdoor@yahoo.com
www.mary-lee-robinson.myshopify.com
www.maryleerobinson.com

Mary Lee Robinson is a native of Towson, Maryland, graduating from high school there and going on to attend Virginia Tech.

Mary Lee has lived in Maryland, Pennsylvania and West Virginia. She now resides in South Carolina, where she retired (she thought) with her husband shortly before his death.

Mary Lee is a Certified Grief Coach, a member of the American Association of Christian Counselors, the author of *The Widow or Widower Next Door,* co-author of *Grief Diaries: Loss of a Spouse*, co-author of *Grief Diaries: How to Help the Newly Bereaved,* and the owner of Rings of Remembrance. She also organizes social clubs for widows and widowers and hopes to see chapters all over the country one day.

\*

PATRICIA SULLIVAN
Patti was 14 when her father Alfred
died at age 61 from a heart attack
Nanamomma2763@hotmail.com

Patti Sullivan was born in 1958, in Massachusetts. Patti's oldest sister was sixteen years her senior, and the closest was seven years her senior. Her older siblings had been raised during their parents' healthy years. Patti was born when her dad lost his health and her mother lost her mind. Patricia's dad was a shoe designer, and the older sisters went to a private school, the household had a maid and a gardener. But Patti's upbringing was humble. Her dad had sixteen operations and took fifty pills a day. When Patti was eight, her mother had a nervous breakdown and was institutionalized on multiple occasions. At the tender age of fourteen, Patti's dad died, leaving her with a mentally ill mother. By her senior year of high school, Patti became pregnant and married. Divorced at an early age, she then remarried and has since celebrated thirty-six years and still going strong. Patti gave birth to three daughters and was given a six-week-old granddaughter to raise. Patti has a certificate in early childhood education and works as a special education para-educator.

\*

JUDY TAYLOR
Judy was 55 when her mum Shirley
died at age 78 from a stroke
www.positivesigns.com.au    \*    posigns@bigpond.net.au

Judy is a mother, sister, daughter, facilitator, speaker, author and an advocate for self-expression. Following a successful sales and marketing background, Judy embraced a more holistic approach to life and found a new and satisfying direction. She began helping her clients embrace their feelings, get to better know themselves and make choices that produced more positive outcomes in their lives. Judy was tested when her mother died suddenly in February 2011. To deal with her grief, Judy began writing her thoughts and feelings down. This provided her with personal comfort and support, and she found friends and colleagues were touched and supported by her words. She was encouraged to share her writings to help others. Her book *MUM MOMENTS – Journey Through Grief* was published in 2014, and her Facebook page by the same name was launched. Both continue to help people around the world who are experiencing the loss of a loved one. Judy's second book, *HEARTSPACE – Letters To My Mother,* is nearing completion. She is passionate about helping and supporting others on their personal journey.

*

ALEXIS VON UTTER
Alexis was 12 when her father Marc
died at age 57 from lung cancer complications

Alexis Von Utter was born in Boynton Beach, Florida. She moved with her family at age three to Maryland. She attended St. Andrew Apostle School from kindergarten until fifth grade, St. Bernadettes School from sixth to eighth grade, Bishop O'Connell High School for her freshman year, and now attends the Academy of the Holy Cross.

Alexis loves to play soccer, basketball, and softball, and she plays competitive softball in high school. She is very fun-loving, enjoys people, and loves to help out.

Alexis works at Chick-fil-A at a mall near her home and loves the interaction she has daily at the register. She loves to tell her story to help others and finds it interesting how many she can heal with it.

\*

HEATHER WALLACE-REY
Heather was 40 when her father John
died suddenly at age 71 of a massive heart attack
www.fivegallonsofcrazy.com  \*  heathercatherine0702@gmail.com

Heather was raised in the suburbs of Chicago and attended Coe College in Cedar Rapids, Iowa. She has been active in ministry for eighteen years and has led workshops that benefit youth and Christian educators. Heather serves on the Annual Events Committee for The Association of Presbyterian Church Educators, has had opportunities to speak at Faith & Grief events (www.faithandgrief.org), and is the Director of Youth Ministries at Second Presbyterian Church in Little Rock, Arkansas.

Heather and her husband David are the parents of the five most wonderful young people in the universe: Ryan, Gordon, Hannah, Nate and Jack, who make her laugh until she cries, daily. Heather enjoys blogging, gardening, public speaking, and spending time with friends and family. Heather's goals in life include being remembered by her family, finding time to vacuum while singing show tunes, being the personal assistant of her favorite children's author (www.gotyourcape.com) and having the opportunity to perform a monologue on the porch of her childhood friend, somewhere in North Carolina, while he pretends not to know her.

Heather is co-author of *Grief Diaries: Loss of a Parent*, and author of *Faith, Grief and Pass The Chocolate Pudding*, due out in 2016.

*There's a bright future for you at every turn,
even if you miss one.*

\*

FROM LYNDA CHELDELIN FELL

# ACKNOWLEDGMENTS

I am deeply indebted to the writers who contributed to *Grief Diaries: Loss of a Parent*. It required a fair bit of time and sometimes tremendous courage to revisit such intimate memories for the purpose of helping others. The collective dedication to seeing this project to the end is a legacy to be proud of.

I very much appreciate author Annah Elizabeth's assistance in framing the start of each chapter. Her positivity and willingness are a breath of fresh air. I'm also grateful to our Grief Diaries village and the very lovely souls I consider dear friends, collaborative partners, mentors, and muses. I treasure each and every one of you!

There simply are no words to express how much I love my husband Jamie, our children, and our wonderfully supportive family and friends for being there through laughter and tears, and encouraging me at every turn. None of this would have been possible without their unquestioning love that continues to surround me.

Finally, I am indebted to our daughter Aly for being my biggest cheerleader in Heaven. Her bright star continues to inspire me, and I can feel her love through the thin veil that separates us as I work to offer help, healing and hope around the world. My dearest Lovey, I love you to the fartherest star and beyond. XO

*Lynda Cheldelin Fell*

Shared joy is doubled joy,
shared sorrow is half a sorrow.
SWEDISH PROVERB

\*

ABOUT

# LYNDA CHELDELIN FELL

Lynda Cheldelin Fell is an international bestselling author, radio and film producer, and inspirational visionary who is passionately dedicated to serving those struggling with life's challenges.

Lynda owns AlyBlue Media, is board president of the National Grief & Hope Coalition, and the creator of the Grief Diaries brand of books, radio, film and webinars. Considered a pioneer in the field of inspirational hope in the aftermath of loss, Lynda creates ground-breaking projects dedicated to raising awareness and compassion, teaching others that they hold the power to change someone's life with just one smile, and inspire hope that life can be full and rich in the aftermath of loss.

Lynda believes that inside every human is a story worth telling, and is passionate about helping people share their journeys through life's most challenging losses.

lynda@lyndafell.com     *     www.LyndaFell.com

*It's important that we share our experiences with other people.*
*Your story will heal you, and your story will heal somebody else.*
*When you tell your story, you free yourself and give other*
*people permission to acknowledge their own story.*
IYANLA VANZANT

\*

To share your story in a Grief Diaries anthology book, visit
www.griefdiaries.com

Published by AlyBlue Media
Inside every human is a story worth sharing.
www.AlyBlueMedia.com

CPSIA information can be obtained
at www.ICGtesting.com
Printed in the USA
FSOW02n0857180316
18182FS